THE STORY OF

USfooty

By

John "Doc" Cheffers

and

Greg Narleski

Officially Requested and Endorsed By The

United States Australian Football League

Copyright 2003 © by John Cheffers
International Standard Book Number: 0-9744403-0-2

All rights reserved.
No part of this book may be used or
reproduced in any form or manner
whatsoever without the written permission
of the author, except that brief passages may
be quoted in critical articles and reviews.

E-mail questions, comments, or suggestions
to johncheffers@msn.com

Printed in the United States of America by
      The Lexington Press, Inc.
      Seven Oakland Street
      Lexington, Massachusetts 02420

INTRODUCTION

BRIAN DIXON[1]

It is an honor to be asked to write the foreword to "The Story of USfooty."

It is a remarkable book and a must for every follower of the game in the USA, Australia, and around the world where the game is played in more than 30 countries.

This book represents a comprehensive account of the growth of Australian football not only in the USA but also in Australia and the 10 other countries that participated in the inaugural international cup in Melbourne, Australia, in 2002.

This book will make a considerable contribution to the development of Australian football in the USA and wherever Australian football is played or will be played. Another vital encouragement will be the links between USA Footy clubs and Leagues and many Australian metropolitan and country Leagues and clubs.

Australian football is a great game. Most Australians believe it is the best game in the world and this is the core reason it deserves to be exposed to the world so that people can have the opportunity of participating in it.

It has some contrasting features with American football. There is no stopping of play or padding of players. Players must think for themselves from all angles. It has unpredictability, long kicking, high marking and is fast flowing. The game had part of its origins based in the Australian Aboriginal game of high marking.

I was fortunate to play for the Melbourne Football Club, the first Australian Football Club formed in 1858. In 1861 the club played exhibition games in New Zealand and in 1963 I played for Melbourne in exhibition games staged in Honolulu and San Francisco against the reigning Australian premiers Geelong.

The book will also find its way to academics of Sport in the USA, Australia and around the world. The latest Academy of Sport to adopt Australian football is the North West Academy of Sport in the North West Province of South Africa.

The AFL is committed to the International Cup being played in Melbourne in 2005 and 2008 and thereafter; probably at four year intervals. The AFL annually commits $A400,000 to assisting the development of the game internationally and this book will be a great support and stimulus to that program.

The book will also stimulate the AFL itself. To survive, Australian Football has to become a truly international sport. The AFL annually turning over $A500 million and a review of its financial contribution internationally will be encouraged by this book.

I look forward to the days when as the authors prophesy, "The day will come when USfooty is financially larger than the AFL."

---

[1] Brian Dixon played 252 games for the Melbourne Football Club (1954-68) and won Club Best and Fairest in 1950. He is an AFL Life Member; Member of the Melbourne Football Club Hall of Fame; Member of the Melbourne Football Club Team of the Century. He starred in five Victorian Football League Premierships and won the Tassie Medal (Best and Fairest at the Australian National Football Carnival) in 1961. He coached North Melbourne Football Club for 44 games and was CEO for the Sydney Swans from 1982 to 1983. He founded the Australian Junior Football Council of Victoria with grants conditional upon support to the Papua New Guinea Australian Football Council.

Brian was a member of the Victorian Parliament representing St. Kilda for 18 years (1964-1982).

TIME FOR REFLECTION

PAUL O'KEEFFE

In our busy society we often do not get or take the time for reflection. What Doc and Greg have created in this book is a chance for us all to reflect on what we have inspired, created and built over the last five to six years. For us "veterans" that have been around since the beginning, it is mind-boggling to reflect on what has happened. As the founder, I am thrilled we have exceeded even my wildest dreams.

This book puts into perspective all the hard work, the political tussles, the harbingers of doom, the victories, the failures, and, most importantly, successes.

Just last week when the Bombers played the Swans, I was talking with one of the original Swans players who played in the first match for either club in early 1998. We were both reminiscing about the "pioneer" days and how much the game has improved.

This book not only tells the stories of how the game has improved on the field, but more importantly tells of how we have matured administratively as a league. Sports administrators around the world, for every sport, take a lot of flak. But, without good administrators, especially visionary ones, sports suffer. This is even more important in the embryonic stage of a sport.

For players who have just been introduced to the sport, or to the expert Aussie who has just gotten off the boat, this book is important as it gives a historical context to where the league has come from. We have our fair share of sins that you may shake your head at but , hopefully, this book will soften your criticism and create a platform for your future involvement in the sport.

In any endeavor such as this there are too many people to personally thank and important people who would be left off any list I could compile. This book will introduce you to many people, or "characters" as Doc loves to say, that have been involved at both the league and club level. Some such as Rich Mann and Sheri Archer, you will come to know and appreciate as Doc and Greg tell their story.

However, I would like to personally thank one person who has had a profound impact on the league beyond what anyone would know or expect. To me he is the unsung hero of the League and represents all the battlers who have made the sport a success. His name is Paul Whiting. During the 1998 annual general meeting, Whitey attended as one of the Boston Demon representatives. This was one of the more highly charged meetings that has taken place in the Leagues' short history. Funnily enough, I attended the meeting with my arm in a sling after it was broken during the Nationals earlier that day. During the meeting it came time for the Leagues' round of formal elections. The group wanted me to continue as President, but I initially declined stating that I would only continue with the support of all the clubs and a full board in place as I could no longer continue as a one-man band. Whitey was the first person to step up and nominate himself. After this act, the tone of the meeting changed and others stepped forward to form the first board. During 1999 Whitey supported my efforts behind the scenes and took a huge portion of the work load off my plate. I firmly believe that without Paul Whiting the story told in this book may have many different outcomes.

Finally, I would like to dedicate my contribution to the USfooty story to my two kids, Heather (9), and David (6). To be able to take my kids to the footy every other Saturday in America is a treat. I know they will grow up with a sense of being Australian, in the most part, due to our great game of footy. They will both grow up involved with me in footy as spectators, players, umpires and fans. That alone makes the journey of the last six years very rewarding.

Thanks Doc and Greg for investing the time and energy to faithfully recording the early years for all to read. I look forward to the 2008 edition to read what happens next.

Paul "Plugger" O'Keeffe
USAFL Founding President
July 2003

THE SKY IS THE LIMIT

By Paul Roos[1]

I became involved with the United States Australian Football League when asked to tour and conduct clinics in the skills and tactics of the game across the country which culminated in my appointment as coach of the American National Team in 1999. They were to play a national team from Canada, in Chicago. Each of the individual clubs in the U.S.A was asked to pick three players for consideration. The criteria for inclusion were twofold: they must either be an American citizen or a green card holder. Eventually, the squad was assembled with 25 players, 19 of whom were American citizens.

The players assembled at a hotel in Chicago ready for a team meeting at 1 pm on a Saturday afternoon in July 1999. Before the game a curtain-raiser exhibition match as was put on by the boys and girls of Komarek Junior High School, sponsored by the Chicago Swans. It was a great thrill to see the junior development program in the U.S. starting to pay dividends. The kids formed an honor guard for the American team which was really pumped up for this its first serious international experience. A physical match resulted with passionate tackling and great enthusiasm displayed under extremely warm conditions. The Americans prevailed by 20 points. Stars on that occasion were Brian Nichol and Donnie Lucero (with only seven games of football behind him).

It was an honor to coach such a committed and passionate group of players and a delight to see their enthusiasm for Australia's national game.

The sky is the limit in the United States.

---

[1] Paul Roos played 356 games with Fitzroy and the Sydney Swans in the AFL in Australia. He is currently coach of the Sydney Swans and is regarded as a premier influence in national as well as international Australian Football matters.

THE AFL SUPPORTS USfooty

One the 7th of February, 2000, the entire football community in the United States received a letter from AFL Chief Executive Office, Wayne Jackson, which was publicized through the Roos network. It read as follows:

"I would like to extend this word of thanks to all those people who have been and are involved in the building of Australian Football in the United States.

All the team at the AFL has watched keenly the growth of the game during the last 2 to 3 years. I personally met with Paul O'Keeffe in December of 1997 as the USAFL was getting underway. It is hard to believe that you are now up to 35 clubs and still growing.

Particularly, this message is to thank those people at the club level who have fueled the grassroots growth of Aussie Rules. For much of the time it is a thankless job and the glory is few and far between. But be assured, you are the glue that holds the structure together. It constantly surprises me the passion that Americans have for our great game and this gives much confidence for the future of the sport Stateside.

We all hope very much you are able to keep up the good work. The AFL plans to continue to support you in your efforts through the national body.

Best of luck with the upcoming season.

Yours sincerely,
W.R. Jackson
Chief Executive Officer
Australian Football League
Melbourne"

ACKNOWLEDGMENTS

The Authors wish to thank the following people for their contributions, great and small.

Plugger O'Keeffe, Richard Mann, Sheri Archer, Greg Everett, Paul Whiting, John "Pops" Meier, Jon Lenicheck, Mark "Wheels" Wheeler, Bill Dusting, Matt Muller, Ken Hawkins, Ron Reed of the <u>Melbourne Herald Sun</u>, Brian Hansen, Brian Dixon, Paul Roos and Andrea Caesar. Unfortunately, the courageous Alma Greeves passed away during the writing of this book.

The AFL, especially, Colin Hutchinson, Wayne Jackson, Ross Smith and Ed Biggs have been very helpful as have the various keepers of the web sites for USAFL clubs.

Incredible computer assistance from Margaret Cheffers, Jean Roberts, Jodie and Matt Beitzel, Judy Gorman and her son Karl, Little One, Michelle and Pat Herrin was given. We must also thank Banjo Paterson and seek his forgiveness for the liberties taken with his outstanding stanzas.

The various officers of the USAFL have given unstintingly as have individuals with whom the authors have conferred.

The saga of USfooty is a story well worth the telling.

John "Doc" Cheffers
Greg Narleski
Boston, June 2003

TABLE OF CONTENTS

Introductory Pages   Page

Introduction:
  Brian Dixon   iii
  Paul O'Keeffe   v
  Paul Roos   vii
Letter from Wayne Jackson   viii
Acknowledgements   ix
Table of Contents   xi
About the Authors   xv

Chapter	Contents	Page
1	CARRYING FOOTY TO THE U.S.A. or 150 YEARS OF FAILURE	1
	The Saga of "Carji" Greeves	9
	The Game Evolves	11
2.	FINALLY SUCCESS	14
	USfooty Club Organizations	16
	Club Website Directories	21
	Website Statistics for 2000	22
	USAFL Income Statement	23
	USAFL Board Members	26
	USfooty Mission Statement	28
3	THOSE RESPONSIBLE	29
	Paul O'Keeffe, Better Known as "Plugger"	29
	Richard Mann	47
	Sheri Archer	54
	Greg Everett	55
	Paul Whiting	58
	USfooty Celebrates	60
	Original Club Pioneers	61
4.	FIVE CHAMPION TEAMS	64
	Cincinnati Dockers	65
	Boston Demons	68

TABLE OF CONTENTS (Cont'd)

Chapter	Contents	Page
	Santa Cruz Roos	74
	Denver Bulldogs	77
	San Diego Lions	80
5	THE WANNABE CHAMPIONS	86
	The Western Region Clubs	88
	The Los Angeles Crows	88
	Orange County Bombers	90
	The Inland Empire Fire	92
	The Phoenix Scorpions/	
	The Arizona Hawks	93
	The Tucson Javelinas	94
	The Seattle Cats now Grizzlies	94
	The Central Region Clubs	96
	Chicago Swans	97
	Chicago Sharks	98
	Dallas Magpies	99
	Detroit Overdrive	100
	Illinois Ironmen	101
	Kansas City Power	101
	Louisville Cats	103
	Milwaukee Bombers	104
	Minnesota Freeze	107
	Nashville Kangaroos	108
	St. Louis Blues	109
	San Antonio Diablos-Austin Crows	110
	Windsor Mariners	111
	Wichita	112
	The Eastern Region Clubs	112
	Atlanta Kookaburras	112
	Baltimore/Washington Eagles	114
	Buffalo	117
	Florida	118
	Green Mountain Eagles	118

TABLE OF CONTENTS (Cont'd)

Chapter	Contents	Page
	The Eastern Region Clubs (Continued)	
	Lehigh Valley Crocodiles	119
	New Hampshire	120
	New York Magpies	120
	North Carolina Tigers	121
	Philadelphia Crows now Hawks	125
	Raleigh	126
	South Carolina Hawks	126
	Tri-Cities Saints	127
	Virginia	128
	Western PA Wallabies	128
6	GEOGRAPHIC DIVISIONS WERE FORMED	129
	The East, Central, West Division Clubs	130
	National Tournament Report	
	- 2002 by John "Pops" Meier	131
	2002 Presidents Report by Jon Lenicheck	136
	2003 Presidents' Incoming Report	
	by Mark Wheeler	141
7	THE REVOLUTION	143
	American Revolution Players for	
	2002 International Cup	145
	Revolution Alternates, Home Clubs	
	Coaching Staff – International Cup 2002	146
	Overseas Born Players – VFL/AFL	147
	Australian Football Around the Globe	150
	Papua New Guinea (The Mosquitoes)	150
	Great Britain (The Bulldogs)	151
	Nauru (The Chiefs)	152
	Japan (The Samurais)	152
	Denmark (The Vikings)	153
	Canada (The Northwind)	153
	Samoa (The Bulldogs)	154
	New Zealand (The Falcons)	155
	South Africa (The Buffaloes)	156
	Ireland	156
	The U.S.A. (The Revolution)	157

TABLE OF CONTENTS (Cont'd)

Chapter	Contents	Page
	THE REVOLUTION (Continued)	
	Games Played	157
	Game 1 – U.S. vs Samoa	157
	Game 2 – U.S. vs New Zealand	158
	Game 3 – U.S. vs Ireland	`159
	Game 4 – U.S. vs Canada	160
	Game 5 – U.S. vs South Africa	160
	Interpool Final	161
	Game 6 – U.S. vs Great Britain	161
	Goal Kickers and Best Players for US Games – 2002 International Cup	162
	International Cup 2002 – Appreciation	164
	International Cup 2002 – Ed Biggs' Report	165
	Final Placings and Awards	167
	Best and Fairest Votes	168
	International Team	169
	The Future	170
	Under 23 Team	171
8	QUO VADIS	172
	Real Footy in the U.S.A.	172
	USAFL Board 2001-2002	175
	USAFL Board 2002-2003	176
	Consolidation	178
	Buildings and Grounds	178
	The National Championships	178
	Sponsorships	179
	Media Attention	179
	AFL Support	179
	What leaps forwards can we expect?	180
	Jealousies	180
	Looking Through the Peephole	180
	REFERENCES	182
	Usfooty teams — Sampling from the *Net*	183
	Excerpts from *Why the Boston Demons play away* – *The Age* October 2, 1999	189

About the Authors

John "Doc" Cheffers is Professor Emeritus at Boston University, President Emeritus of AIESEP and Fellow of AIESEP. He played with The Kew Baptist Football Club (2 years), Kew Amateurs A Grade, (one year), Carlton (one year) and Box Hill (4 years). A career ending knee injury at the age of 20 sent him limping into the ranks of coaching and  managing, an area where he has enjoyed the ambience. He has been on the Boston Demons Board for five years.

 Greg Narleski is President of the Boston Demons Football Club. Greg has played for five years with the team and represented the USA Revolution Team that played in London in 2001. Greg is a Doctoral student at Boston University.

THE STORY OF USfooty

Chapter 1

CARRYING "FOOTY" TO THE U.S.A.

Or

150 Years of Failure

The pristine city of Melbourne was founded late by Australian standards. Sydney had been founded in 1778 and Hobart, not long afterwards. Melbourne, at the base of the Australian mainland, was not formed until 1833, but it did not take long for Melbournians to be heard. The title of Crown City in the new State of Victoria was in doubt through the 1850's. The port of Geelong and the tent city of Ballarat fifty miles inland, for a short while, vied for top city in Victoria. Ballarat's credentials were not hard to find – an old school teacher called Nathan Spielvogul endowed the reasons in verse:

"In '51 a tale was told
In many a town in Europe old,
Of a new found pasture town with gold
Ho! Ho! Have ye heard of Ballarat?

"Come bid farewell and sail away,
Sail and sail for a hundred day,
Across the sea to Hobson's Bay
Away and away to Ballarat."

Quoted in C. C. Mullen, <u>History of Australian Football</u>.

The gold flooded the fields around Ballarat and a neighboring town called Bendigo. Melbourne was the point on the triangle sixty miles from these two cities and became the focal point for banking and business. It was in this fair city that civilization sprang up in short time.

By 1859, a new game had developed which soon became known as "Australian Rules" and, not surprisingly, two intrepid Irishmen were credited with its beginnings. Principal culprit was Tom Wills – a serious-minded entrepreneur, described as dapper and sensitive and called "the man with zingari stripe," which referred to a shirt he wore with distinctive and striped colors. He was educated in England where he played football and cricket and every other game he could. Upon his return to Melbourne with another more fractious and loquacious Irishman named Harrison, he began the game.

Folklore has it that five or six games were played in Melbourne every year since 1840, but the first officially recorded match took place on August 7th, 1858, between Scotch College and Melbourne Grammar School in Yarra Park. Stories differ about this distinct occasion, but the flavor is rich. Apparently, the ground was so long that when standing at one goal line, it was impossible to see the goal at the other. Tom Wills was reputed to have been one of the umpires and the game, played all Saturday afternoon, ended in a draw so the teams returned two Saturdays later to play for a result.

This full day's play failed to separate the teams, so they returned again two weeks later and finding a similar result declared the game drawn. Perhaps this game explains why its competitive brother, cricket, sees its players play for five consecutive days to achieve the same result – a draw. One month before this game on July 10th, the Melbourne Football Club was formed. In 1859 Geelong formed a club, with Carlton following in 1864, North Melbourne in 1869 and between 1872 and 1884, Essendon, St. Kilda, South Melbourne, Footscray, Fitzroy and Richmond formed clubs. With the formation of Collingwood in 1892, most of the inner suburbs of Melbourne claimed a team and it could truthfully be said that this unique and wonderful game was contained within Melbourne suburbs for almost one hundred years.

Attempts were made to break out. In 1876, the game was established in New Zealand. Before that in 1867, Tasmania saw the game begin. About that time, South Australia and Western Australia adopted Australian Football as their primary winter game.

The unlikely town of Dunedin (NewZealand) saw two clubs formed in 1876. Ominously, in 1870, the game of rugby was introduced to New Zealand and quickly became popular. Australian Football, however, took hold and was played seriously until 1913 when a test series was held with Victoria. Serious differences between the two teams destroyed this initiative and the game died in New Zealand from that time on.

Australian "footy" was played in the southern part of New South Wales seriously, especially in Albury and Wagga Wagga but it became a recreational pastime in Sydney and Brisbane due to the prominence of Rugby League and Union.

About this time, the vicissitudes of transport were illustrated with the story of St. Kilda sending a team to play South Australia by sea in 1877. Connection with the Australians' literary world occurred with a commemorative game played to honor Marcus Clarke in 1881. Clarke was the author of the very famous novel "For the Term of His Natural Life." Not unlike Tom Wills who died broke, Marcus Clarke was penniless and at his premature death a game was played to raise money for his widow and children.

In the same year, Geelong considered playing exhibition games in England and, by 1893, there were forty-four clubs established in New Zealand. In the 1890's, with the gold streams drying up in Victoria, diggers spread out to South Africa, England and Scotland taking the game with them. Unfortunately, like trees planted in shallow soil, their roots withered and the trees died. AFL archivist, Colin Hutchinson puts it this way:

> "There were quite viable competitions in existence in New Zealand and South Africa prior to World War 1. From the 1890's through to the outbreak of World War 1, it's believed that the main reason those competitions started up was because of gold rushes in both New Zealand and South Africa where Australian gold fossickers, or people in the industry followed their dreams. When the industry petered out somewhat in Australia they migrated either to New Zealand or South Africa to continue their trade and probably took the game with them, yet with the outbreak of World War 1 many of those people joined the military forces. Unfortunately the competitions tended to wane from that point."

In 1859, United States businessmen contemplated taking the game back to the U.S. with some serious intent. They negotiated with four clubs – Melbourne, Essendon, Geelong and South Melbourne. The scheme looked promising, but with the collapse of banks and businesses around this time, the idea was abandoned. Several diggers from Victoria went to the United States as the gold was drying up and actually formed clubs in

Detroit, Boston, St. Louis, Philadelphia, Oakland and San Francisco. They called these clubs, variously, Victoria, Melbourne, Wattles, Kangaroos, Southern Cross, Batman, Fawkner, Royal Park, Magpies, Port Philip, Collingwood and Yarra Town. They financed the clubs themselves and played vigorously. Their success varied but soon collapsed. Leaders in the U.S. were impressed with this fast and furious game which was free of serious injuries. These promising earlier attempts failed because they mostly consisted of ex-patriots playing the game they loved and because they returned to Australia when financial conditions improved. The necessary groundwork of organization and financing did not occur. Some subsidiary efforts sputtered on. Youth clubs sprang up in Seattle, San Francisco and Wisconsin where university students became involved.

In 1895, the game almost took off in the United States. President Teddy Roosevelt expressed great alarm at the serious injuries and deaths occurring in American Football in club matches and university games – such friendly habits as the "flying wedge" contributed to these deaths. In order to break up the wall of players in front of them, teams would hold an individual horizontal and ram his stiff body headfirst into the opposition team. This unkind action contributed more than anything else to Teddy Roosevelt's disillusionment with his national game. He cast around for an alternative and indeed gave the Presidential order, "clean it up or I'll close it down". The Americans saved their game with the genius of the forward-pass which opened a trail to goal and introduced a most exciting facet to their national game. But the Victorian Football League, to its credit, took the initiative and sent the following letter to the U.S. President:

> "To The Honorable President of the United States of America,
> Mr. Theodore Roosevelt,
>
> Sir,--Noting in the press that you had expressed yourself as to the desirability of some alteration in the rules of football as played in the United States of America, the Victorian Football League desires to most respectfully submit to you copies of the Laws of the Australasian game.
> The Australasian code was founded in Victoria and is now played in all States of the Commonwealth as well as in New Zealand, South Africa and overseas, and in all schools, colleges and universities.
> One of the greatest advantages which will appeal to you most

strongly is the comparative immunity from serious accidents to players, the laws having been so framed and revised from time to time so that while maintaining its character as a strong, healthy vigorous and manly sport, it is a game wherein all have an equal chance, as science and skill predominates and not brute strength.

Our lands are not far apart, and we can but fervently hope that matches on an International character may yet eventuate.

Australia has given many good ideas to the world, and we are happy to still further contribute to the sport and pleasure of our cousins in America our evolution of the laws of a great game of football, the game of today and the future. We are a young nation, but all the elements that lead to prosperity and magnitude are present. We know that your people are always ready to grasp and hold to anything that is good, and this we offer to you in our own game."

At the same time, the League wrote to 69 universities and secondary schools in the States, selling the praises of the Australian game. Unfortunately, the necessary infrastructure of local presence and follow-up was not understood at that time, so the attempts withered and failed. In 1908, the U.S. Fleet visited Australia and were awed by this game, but words of praise amounted to faint praise in the establishment of the game. In 1909, Major Pierotto and Garnet Holm brought 60 U.S. schoolboys, aged 14-18 years, to Australia for an educational visit. Part of their brief was to learn the Australian game and play matches. This they did against college teams and Melbourne area schools. They played a combined team from north of the Yarra and one from south of the Yarra. They even played a curtain raiser at an Essendon VFL game on the old and famous East Melbourne ground. The two leaders were enthusiastic and upon their return to the U.S., organized a number of schools with teams and competitions to play. The game looked like spreading – unfortunately the outbreak of World War 1, dealt a death blow and the efforts floundered.

In 1896, a new institution was formed in Melbourne. The old group, the VFA (the Victorian Football Association), had controlled football to this time. The better teams, tired of the constrictions of the VFA, split and formed the VFL (Victorian Football League) which soon became the premier organization. But this split, along with the independence of the various country leagues in Victoria, heralded in a chronic and debilitating war that sapped the efforts of administrators and organizers. With the leaders occupied in this internecine combat, little thought was given to expanding the game overseas. A fledging organization called the Australian Football League was formed with former Collingwood player Bruce Andrew as its director. Andrew often rued the inward-looking posture of this group and spent most of his time writing on the skills and the rules of this game. His rationale was that this information would be needed when the game began to spread.

In 1911, Harry Bromley bounced a "Sherrin" football on the east coast of the U.S... He had been busily discussing the game with the sporting fold in that country, witnessing local American games and interviewing their leading players. Bromley's efforts faded with a conclusion that the quality of the Sherrin football was superior to the American version. In 1914, a Mr. J. Smith presented his plan to the Australian Football Council to take a team to America. Nothing further is known of this intention. WW I, apart from two fascinating tidbits, stunted the growth of the Australian game almost completely. In 1917, Lieutenant L. G. Short, an "Argus" journalist, wrote to his old paper about a football match held in France on a snow-covered, shell-pitted ground won from the enemy, but still within artillery range. The NCO's defeated the officers of an Australian battalion played in a game precariously around unexploded shell holes, the goal posts at one end consisted of a small heap of Earth believed to have contained the graves of dead soldiers. Short made issue of the great fun that was had that day before they returned to the front lines. The second story, much better documented, consisted of the famous ANZAC's match in London on October 28th, 1916, played on the Queen's Club Ground in West Kensington. Three thousand people reached high pitch in enthusiasm as the Third Division defeated the Training Groups 6-16 to 4-12. Many well-known Australian League and Association footballers are documented as playing in this game. Two, Bruce Sloss, who captained the Third Division team and J. Cooper who featured with the Training Units team, were soon to be killed in action in the trenches in France.

A fascinating story was found concerning a little known Australian footballer who was to be a star in the U.S. at the American grid-iron games. His name was Patrick O'Dea. From 1893-95, he played for Melbourne and Essendon. Born in Kilmore on March 17, 1876, Patrick attended Kew College (later Xavier College) excelling at scholarship and in rowing, swimming, athletics and football. He migrated to America upon graduation to study law at the University of Wisconsin – naturally he played grid iron. The American game permitted three points to be scored when a drop-kick went over the cross bar between the two goal posts. This method of scoring was rare as few Americans could perform a drop-kick on the run under tackling pressure from the opponents. O'Dea dominated the game so much in his five playing seasons that the Americans changed the rules and accorded this practice only one point. Even O'Dea astounded the Americans with his capacity to drop-kick goals. He shunned publicity, changed his name to Charles Mitchell and served with the U.S. army during WW I. Eventually his true identity surfaced, forcing him to emerge from obscurity in September, 1954. The Americans hailed him as one of the champions of their game, inducting him into the American Football Hall of Fame when it was first established in 1962.

In 1925, the American visiting fleet enthusiastically viewed a game between Essendon and Collingwood at the old ground in Victoria Park. In 1932, the VFL demonstrated a prime reason why football did not emigrate to the U.S. for so many years. A proposal to send a team to play in the States at the end of 1933 was put forward after the story of Mr. Eric Cullenwood, a former Australian player then resident in California,. and his establishment of Field Ball was introduced. Apparently, the game became so popular that young Australian boys visited and played against a competent American team and its popularity caused a half-day holiday to be declared for the first game. The League rejected this idea on the ground that the time was inopportune and the move would not help the game. Opposing the notion, delegate Mr. G. Cathie said it was extremely doubtful whether grounds large enough could be obtained and another delegate, Mr. T. Rush said it was too early and when the time was right, it should be introduced by boys of The Young Australian League. Oh dear!!!

In 1943, an unusual competition took place. Bill Jost, an American serviceman and former grid-iron player for the Huntington Golden Bears, regained his title as "longest propeller of football in the free world." He first lost the title when Fred Hughson of Fitzroy drop-kicked a football 83 yards 11 inches, measured against Jost's throws at close to 70 yards. At an ensuing carnival, North Melbourne's Alf Hacker managed a drop-kick of 62 yards, but lost to Jost's throw of 63 yards, 1 foot. The contest caused much discussion but did little to further the cause of spreading footy to the United States. In 1944, however, many Australian footballs were taken around the world and the game was demonstrated in the course of World War II collegiality. Comment on the success of these ventures appeared in Canadian newspapers and among the annals of such notable sporting conglomerations as the Helms Athletic Foundation in New York.

Sporadic information lead to the V.F.L. in 1947 contemplating sending league teams to play U.S. exhibition matches and in 1963, Geelong and Melbourne played two exhibition matches against each other in Honolulu and San Francisco. AFL historian, Colin Hutchinson, has this to say about these games:

> "In one of the matches there was quite a violent fight break out and players were taking the game very seriously at the time. The players were best of mates during the trip itself but for this hour or so during the exhibition if "investigation by video" had been in operation I'm sure that half the payers wouldn't have made a start to the 1964 season. They had some very good crowds to those matches, in fact, I don't have it in my direct possession, but I know there is some movie footage of some of that tour where it shows some of the match action, some of the crowd scenes and, I think, there are even a few interviews with some of the personalities of the two teams."

In 1980, the U.S. Cable TV Network (ESPN) paid the VFL US$100,000 for the rights to broadcast "the match of the day." In 1988, Collingwood defeated Geelong in Miami and Essendon defeated Hawthorn one year later in the same U.S. city. In 1990, Melbourne defeated West Coast in Portland, USA and, by 1995, the Australian Football Association of North America was founded. The ten previous years had seen multiple touring games played by Australian League teams in many countries around the globe. There is little doubt that the tactic was succeeding for the Canadian Australian Football Association (founded in 1989) and the British Australian Football League (founded in 1990) preceded the founding of the Danish Australian Football League in 1991. Soon after, the International Australian Football Council was founded in 1995 and with member nations competing at the biennial Arafura Games. These members consisted of Japan, Singapore, Hong Kong, Nauru, Papua New Guinea and New Zealand. Not long afterwards, the Singapore Wombats, the Jakarta Bintangs, the Central Desert Eagles, the Malaysia Tigers and Bali added their names to the growing list of Australian Football aficionados.

International competitions were now springing up all over the world. In October 2001, a round robin competition named The Atlantic Alliance Cup, between Denmark-Sweden, Great Britain, Ireland, Canada and the U.S.A. took place in London. Feature of this competition was the ruling that only players of national birth could be members of the respective teams. Although the presence of Australian ex-patriots would enhance the quality of play, it was correctly deduced that the national teams should consist of local identities. The "State of Origin" concept was with us.

Ron Barassi's prophecies of 1977 were fast materializing.

> "Don't laugh" Barassi warned, "the thrill of a fully national competition or even semi-international atmosphere, could well inspire a real concerted attempt to bring Ireland and maybe the West Coast of America into our football field" he predicted.

And remember, when Barassi so prophesied, the then VFL was nothing more than a twelve team state league, with its torrid suburban identities.

In 1995, Nick Garifalakis reported on the efforts of a teacher in Chicago's western suburbs, to develop the game. He was Jeff Norris, a History and Physical Education teacher at Komarek School on the shores of Lake Michigan. He was first exposed to Australian football ten years earlier when watching a game between Collingwood and Hawthorn on cable TV. Using the video tapes and a book by U.S. based author Peter Maddern called "Australian Rules – The Complete Guide," Norris set out to introduce the game to his students. Carlton and Richmond offered assistance. He organized a summer camp which was attended by 150 students and continued evangelizing the game at the Illinois State Sport Convention the next year. Its success continues. By 1997, twenty-five Komarek High School girls and boys visited Australia at the hosting of Ivanhoe Grammar. Mark Neeld, a former Richmond player, is a teacher there and continues his support for the Chicago ensemble. The visitors entertained patrons at half-time during the Geelong Richmond game in that season. The Australian sponsors continued the exchange of audio and video tapes to the Americans at that time and had educated thousands of Americans in so doing.

The Saga of "Carji" Greeves

On a typical wind-strewn, stormy Melbourne winter day, the authors visited the gracious 96-year-old widow of Carji Greeves. She lives in a hillside cottage nestled in the lovely hills of Anglesea on the South western coast of Victoria. She was lucid, clear and very credible and she talked about her famous husband, his playing days with the Geelong Football Club and especially his six-month visit to the US in 1928. A brilliant player with Geelong, Carji played 124 games and in the premiership teams of 1925 and 1931 and had the distinction of being the first Brownlow medalist in Australian football, awarded in 1924, but he finished second in the counting in 1925, 1926, and 1928 and fourth in 1927. A severe knee injury in 1930 hampered his playing career thereafter but did not stop him from continuing through 1933. His nickname "Carji" had originated from an entertainer named "Carjilo – the Prince of Bong" who was the big hit in Geelong when Carji began his career.

His kicking style was classic, causing him to be invited to the US to instruct grid-iron players at the University of Southern California in the art of kicking. Immediately upon his arrival at USC he made many friends among officials and players, but his advice on kicking took some time before it was accepted. This reluctance was due mainly to the insistence by US coaches at that time that the ball be kicked by the toe rather than from the instep of the foot. His original time of four months was extended so that players could experience his facility of kicking more prodigiously, but Greeves also shrewdly assessed the needs for establishing the code in USA. Australian Football was continuous, rather than interrupted, as grid-iron continues to be today. As the plays are more deliberate, there is an absence of the spontaneous deep-throated roar that comes from thousands of Australian barrackers with the vicissitudes of the play in Australian Football. Frankly, the game is highly unpredictable. Col Hutchinson agrees." The only aspect of Australian Football which is predictable is its increasing rate of unpredictability."

The American game was marred by many deaths at this time causing thoughtful Americans to wonder if some less harmful game could be found. The college game was supreme when Carji played in the States, so he saw the need for tours to be organized through the university systems. In those days, the US professional teams had little money and small crowds, so the leading players were amateur and the support better organized. Carji also recognized that the habit of describing a game over loudspeakers, while in progress, would be an effective way of selling it to the people. Carji returned to Australia, won another premiership with Geelong in 1931 and retired in 1933 - his US efforts remain enshrined in a small pleasant home in the hills of Anglesea.

His trip was not without some distinct advantages. The US flew Carji to the oil fields around California and upon his return he was employed with the same company. Alma Greeves relishes the story of Carji winning his first Brownlow medal:

> "He was only twenty when he came directly from Geelong College to play with Geelong when he won his medal. I was eighteen at the time, so I don't have long memories of that time…He didn't go to play American Football, rather to teach them how to kick…I believe they were kicking about forty yards, Carji was successful in bringing up that distance to sixty yards."

She rued his early death at sixty and frankly placed some of the blame on to the rigors of the game. Her thoughts were positive, though, on her husband's illustrious career and she enjoyed the hour we spent with her on this blustery Melbourne winter's day.

The point of Carji's experience in this story is that the ball was left once again standing in the centre of the oval with Australian Football no closer to taking hold in the U.S. President Teddy Roosevelt had suggested the American game was too rough. Twenty-six-years later, Carji Greeves reported that there were still many deaths in grid-iron – but a culture tends to cling to its own makings. And although successful, grid-iron was promoted with the colleges and defense academies at this time with the professional lagging in the rear, Americans persisted with their game and attractive intruders like Australian Football, Soccer, Rugby and Gaelic Football had to be content with far fewer opportunities and far less recognition.

The Game Evolves

As the game continues to spread across the globe, the influence of the internet has given an impetus that resembles the tortoise and the hare. We had turtley torpor for 150 years; today we have the rapid fire of the speedy hare. And the game itself evolves. Colin Hutchinson reminds us of some of these changes in the history of Australian Football:

> "In the very early days of Australian Football when the first set of codified rules was drawn up, the playing field was rectangular." He continues, "And even though there were behind posts, as well as goal posts, behinds did not count in the score until 1897." He talked then about the ball, "Originally a spherical ball was used, rather than an oval shaped one which is fascinating when compared with Gaelic Football. The Irish game was first played with an oval ball and they

switched to a spherical one about the time when we changed to an oval ball. I have a theory, which I don't have much evidence to support, but gives me something to think about – perhaps in the 1800's the technology was lacking and the balls did not retain their shape, perhaps some of the spherical balls became misshapen creating the fun of the unpredictable bounce so people started to think this is the best ball to play with, so let's deliberately manufacture oval balls."

[i]Col Hutchinson's theory on the origins of high marking is very credible.

"When Australian Football was developed by Thomas Wills, it's believed he used the elements of the aboriginal game 'marngrook', I have some literature on that. Now in 'marngrook' the main element is the use of the ball, usually made from animal skins stuffed with either charcoal or feathers. The participants of the game just gathered together with the game starting when someone kicked the ball as high into the air as he could and the objective was for each participant to try to catch the ball. The winner was rewarded by being allowed to take the next kick. There was no scoring or not rules as such but that was the primary idea of the game. It's fascinating that in one of the aboriginal dialects the word 'mark' actually means 'catch'. So perhaps that's where the word 'mark' in Australian Football came from. Some people dispute that and say well perhaps it was to do with people catching the ball and marking the spot on the ground, but I tend to go along with the first explanation. In the early 1800's a champion Essendon footballer named Charlie Pearson, is credited by some people with inventing the high mark, but I tend to think that perhaps he popularized it. He perhaps became a great exponent of it and developed a technique which was probably better than the technique used by other players and therefore he was given a lot of publicity about taking high marks, but I think high marks probably were in football well before that anyway."

Hutchinson has a story illustrating yet another feature of the Australian game – umpire baiting:

"There's an interesting anecdote going back to 1924 when St. Kilda played Carlton at Princess Park and on that particular day St. Kilda seemed to be getting the wrong end of the stick when it came to umpiring decisions, all the free kicks and awarded marks seemed to be going Carlton's way. And the St. Kilda captain of the day who's name was Wells Eicke, was complaining to the umpire and saying well come on give us a fair go we've only had three free kicks and Carlton's had ten already, and he kept at the umpire all day and the umpire was telling him to keep quiet and get on with the game. At one stage Wells Eicke called the umpire over and said I want you to stop the game the opposition has too many players on the field at the moment, so under the rules of the game the umpire has to take notice of the captain who requests such account. So the game was stopped, and the Carlton team was lined up and the umpire commenced counting the players. He went up and down the line 1, 2, 3, 4, 5 etc. etc. 16, 17, 18 so then he turned to Wells Eicke and said Wells you're wrong, there is the designated number of players here, 18 Carlton players on the field, so we'll get on with the game, and Wells Eicke said 'hang on a minute, you haven't counted yourself yet'."

---

[i] The authors are grateful to USAFL Archivist, Col Hutchinson, for assembling notes about the beginnings of Australian Football. These sources are both known and unknown.

THE STORY OF USfooty
CHAPTER 2

FINALLY SUCCESS

For many years droves of conscientious people endeavored to bring Australian Football to the United States, but none succeeded. Co-author, Greg Narleski, is asking the central question for his Doctoral Dissertation at Boston University, "Why, after 150 years of failure is Australian Football finally deriving permanence, why is it sticking today?" Several reasons have been discovered as the research for this book unfolded. Gritty pioneers like Paul O'Keeffe and Richard Mann, together with a number of other stalwarts, have gone to work. We will look at their backgrounds to uncover reasons for their persistence. A host of other players have entered this game with helpful and vital contributions: they will all be discussed in due time also. The infrastructure, which is so needed for a game to develop permanence, was laid in the 1990's and is continuing at breakneck speed into this century. The internet, with its capacity for instant and global communication, is a vital cause for this achievement. The Australian Football League (AFL) has embraced the cause with enthusiasm and generosity. The stingy Victorian Football League (VFL) of the 1930's, which refused to vote any monies for expansion, is now in the distant past. In 2001, the AFL voted AU$120,000 to the central authorities in the United States: unfortunately, the Australian dollar, being at fifty per cent of the American dollar, has meant severe weakening of this support. The very nature of the original sum, however, is clearly indicative that support is now available in Australia. Indeed, in 2002, eleven countries sent representative teams to Melbourne in August to compete in what is now called "The International Cup." The presence of so many countries sporting Australian Football teams evidences clearly the effect of the expansion worldwide.

Another reason that Australian Football is now a viable entity in the United States is the support it is generating from the market place. The Adelaide Brewery, Coopers, and the Victorian winery, McPhersons, have led the charge. Whereas most initial marketing ventures originated in Victoria, the spread of the game to other states and countries has meant that new competitors with expanded objectives have entered the fray. The

Sherrin Football, for instance, along with "Match" dominated the production of balls until "Burley" began expanding from its Western Australian base. The ball is one of the most viable features of the Australian game, so the presence of an interloper from Perth added zest to the commercial enterprise. The evidence supporting the general enthusiasm for USfooty permanence comes from three distinct sources: first, the USfooty Handbook of 2000; second, the Program for the 2001 National Championships in Maryland and third, the USAFL 2000 Annual Report

And it is time to draw the verifying statistics from these sources. Table 2-1 shows a map of the US with Burley Sekem footballs placed in the various cities and areas. Table 2-2 lists the vital information on 32 of the current clubs. Table 2-3 lists the website directory of the USAFL and Table 2-4 lists the web site statistics for USfooty. Further damning evidence is contained in Table 2-5 where the USAFL Income Statement is outlined.

The year 2001 represented the fifth year of modern USfooty. A number of important developments occurred during this year. First, a conference was held in April in what has become the founding city of USfooty, Cincinnati. It was synonymous with dangerous race riots at the time and the USAFL met to determine the future of USfooty. The program consisted of workshops dealing with the constitution, membership application, club administration, junior development, umpire development, sponsorship, coach and player development and the national tournament. Thirty of the 32 teams sent delegates from teams at various stages of maturity. Clubs like Boston, Nashville, New York, Denver, Santa Cruz, San Diego, Seattle, Chicago and Cincinnati had been established for most of the life of USfooty, but teams like Philadelphia, Phoenix, Portland, Florida, San Antonio and Minnesota were described as "under development."

TABLE 1
USFOOTY CLUB ORGANIZATIONS

Western Region
- Denver Bulldogs
- Inland Empire Eagles
- Los Angeles Crows
- Orange County Bombers
- Phoenix Scorpions
- Portland/Oregon
- San Diego Lions
- Santa Cruz Roos
- Seattle Cats

Central Region
- Chicago Swans
- Cincinnati Dockers
- Dallas Magpies
- Detroit Overdrive
- Illinois Ironmen
- Kansas City Power
- Louisville Cats
- Milwaukee Bombers
- Minnesota Freeze
- Nashville Kangaroos
- St. Louis Blues
- San Antonio

Eastern Region
- Atlanta Kookaburras
- Baltimore/Washington Eagles
- Boston Demons
- Buffalo
- Florida
- Lehigh Valley Crocodiles
- New York Magpies
- North Carolina Tigers
- Philadelphia Crows
- South Carolina Hawks
- Tri Cities Saints

USFOOTY
United States Australian Football League

TABLE 2
INFORMATION ON 32 OF CURRENT CLUBS

Football Clubs — Eastern Region

Atlanta Kookaburras

Atlanta Kookaburras Australian Football Club
550 McWhorter Drive
Atlanta, GA 30606

Web Address: www.atlantafooty.com
email: npowers@qualcomm.com

Sister Club: Richmond Tigers

Baltimore/Washington Eagles

 **Baltimore/Washington DC Eagles Australian Football Club**
2516 Strathmore Avenue
Baltimore, MD 21214

Web Address: www.baltimoredceagles.com
email: azrules@baltimoredceagles.com

Sister Club: West Coast Eagles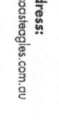

Boston Demons

Boston Demons Australian Football Club
P.O. Box 390086
Cambridge, MA 02139

Web Address: www.bostondemons.org
email: demons@bostondemons.org

Sister Club: Melbourne Demons

Buffalo — Under Development

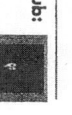 **Buffalo VFC Australian Football Club**
60 Ladner Avenue
Buffalo, NY 14220

Web Address: www.usfooty.com
email: earl3939@hotmail.com

Football Clubs — Eastern Region

Florida — Under Development

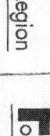 **Florida Australian Football Club**
5521 47th CT E
Bradenton, FL 34203

Web Address: www.usfooty.com
email: jkeustice@aol.com

Lehigh Valley Crocodiles

 **Lehigh Valley Crocodiles Australian Football Club**
20 E. North Street
Nazareth, PA 18064

Web Address: www.lvcrocs.com
email: rmgia@yahoo.com

Sister Club: Hampton Rovers

New York Magpies

 **New York Magpies Australian Football Club**
21-18 45th Street
Lic, NY 11101

Web Address: www.nyfooty.com
email: president@nyfooty.com

Sister Club: Collingwood Magpies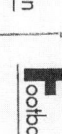

North Carolina Tigers

 **North Carolina Tigers Australian Football Club**
416 H Hensley Drive
Raleigh, NC 27615

Web Address: www.nctigers.com
email: nctigers@hotmail.com

Sister Club: Richmond Tigers

TABLE 2
INFORMATION ON 32 OF CURRENT CLUBS (Continued)

Eastern Region

Philadelphia Crows

Philadelphia Crows Australian Football Club
220 Wayne Avenue
Haddonfield, NJ 08033

Web Address: http://phillycrows.homestead.com
email: cwhasson@home.com

Sister Club:
Adelaide Crows
Web Address:
www.afc.com.au

South Carolina Hawks

South Carolina Hawks Australian Football Club
201 Robinson Street
Greenville, SC 29609

Web Address: www.members.home.com/rodders/schawks/index.htm
email: tonymahar@hotmail.com

Sister Club:
Richmond Tigers
Web Address:
www.richmondfc.com.au

Tri-Cities Saints

Tri-Cities Saints Australian Football Club
510 Jim Elliot Road
Johnson City, TN 37601

Web Address: www.usfooty.com
email: warrenballagh@chartertn.net

Sister Club:
St. Kilda Saints
Web Address:
www.stkilda.afl.com.au

Central Region

Chicago Swans

Chicago Swans Australian Football Club
3238 S. Highland Avenue
Berwyn, IL 60402-3514

Web Address: www.chicagoswans.com
email: julescallachan@yahoo.com

Sister Club:
Sydney Swans
Web Address:
www.sydneyswans.com.au/2000/swansflash.htm

Cincinnati Dockers

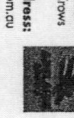

Cincinnati Dockers Australian Football Club
2982 Linwood Avenue, 3rd Floor
Cincinnati, OH 45208

Web Address: www.cincinnatidockers.com
email: president@cincinnatidockers.com

Sister Club:
Fremantle Football Club
Web Address:
www.dockers.com.au

Dallas Magpies

Dallas Magpies Australian Football Club
402 Inglewood Drive
Richardson TX 75080

Web Address: www.usfooty.com
email: mmanoel@texascustompools.com

Sister Club:
Collingwood Magpies
Web Address:
www.collingwoodfc.com.au

Detroit Overdrive

Detroit Overdrive Australian Football Club
470 E. Elmwood, Suite 201
Clawson, MI 48017

Web Address: www.detroitfootyclub.com
email: information@detroitfootyclub.com

TABLE 2
INFORMATION ON 32 OF CURRENT CLUBS (Continued)

Football Clubs — Central Region

Illinois Ironmen

Illinois Ironmen Australian Football Club
530 Country Club Lane
Itasca, IL 60143

Web Address: www.usfooty.com
email: chodwg1@cs.com

Kansas City Power

Kansas City Power Australian Football Club
5228 Bond Street
Shawnee, KS 66203

Web Address: www.kcpower.com
email: info@kcpower.com

Sister Club: Port Adelaide Power
Web Address: www.portpower.com/au

Louisville Cats

Louisville Cats, Australian Football Club
1706 Devondale Driver
Louisville, KY 40222

Web Address: www.usfooty.com
email: louisville_fc@hotmail.com

Sister Club: Geelong Cats
Web Address: www.gfc.com.au

Milwaukee Bombers

Milwaukee Bombers Australian Football Club
5920 W. Wisconsin Avenue
Milwaukee, WI 53213

Web Address: www.milwaukeebombers.com
email: info@milwaukeebombers.com

Sister Club: Essendon Bombers
Web Address: www.essendonfc.com.au

Football Clubs — Central Region

Minnesota Freeze *Under Development*

Minnesota Freeze Australian Football Club
15000 Tyacke Drive
Burnsville, MN 55306

Web Address: www.usfooty.com
email: adavis@larsonallen.com or freeze@pucknet.com

Nashville Kangaroos

Nashville Kangaroos Australian Football Club
P.O. Box 128156
Nashville, TN 37212

Web Address: www.nashvillekangaroos.org
email: info@nashvillekangaroos.org

Sister Club: Kangaroos Football Club
Web Address: www.ozemail.com.au

St. Louis Blues

Saint Louis Blues Australian Football Club
870 Liongate
St. Louis, MO 63130

Web Address: www.bluesfooty.com
email: jmartin@lewisrice.com

Sister Club: Carlton Blues
Web Address: www.carltonfc.com.au

San Antonio *Under Development*

San Antonio Australian Football Club
18015 Redriver Song Road
San Antonio, TX 78259

Web Address: www.usfooty.com
email: steve@clockworkdesign.com

TABLE 2
INFORMATION ON 32 OF CURRENT CLUBS (Continued)

Football Clubs ●●● — Western Region

Denver Bulldogs

Denver Bulldogs Australian Football Club
6046 S. Pierson Street
Littleton, CO 80127

Web Address: www.denverbulldogs.com
email: doinouski.mott@broadband.att.net

Sister Club: Western Bulldogs
Web Address: www.westernbulldogs.com.au

Inland Empire Eagles

Inland Empire Eagles Australian Football Club
1201 University Avenue, #106
Riverside, CA 92507

Web Address: www.eaglefooty.com
email: salesoagis@earthlink.net

Sister Club: West Coast Eagles
Web Address: www.westcoasteagles.com.au

Los Angeles Crows

Los Angeles Crows Australian Football Club
815 Magnolia Street
South Pasadena, CA 91030

Web Address: www.lacrows.com
email: info@lacrows.com

Orange County Bombers

Orange County Bombers Australian Football Club
147 Cozumel G9
Laguna Beach, CA 92651

Web Address: www.ocbombers.com
email: info@ocbombers.com

Sister Club: Essendon Bombers
Web Address: www.essendonfc.com.au

Football Clubs ●●● — Western Region

Phoenix Scorpions

Phoenix Scorpions Australian Football Club
7998 E. Via Bonita
Scottsdale, AZ 85258

Web Address: www.phoenixscorpions.com
email: info@phoenixscorpions.com

Sister Club: Springvale Scorpions
Web Address: www.springvalefootballclub.com.au

Portland/Oregon *Under Development*

Portland/Oregon Australian Football Club
255 East Dartmouth Street
Gladstone, OR 97027

Web Address: www.usfooty.com
email: scott_johnson@mentorg.com or kjvlpl@msn.com

San Diego Lions

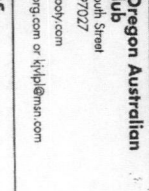

San Diego Lions Australian Football Club
8889 Caminiolo Plaza Centro #7423
San Diego, CA 92122

Web Address: www.sandiegolions.com
email: sandiegolions@email.com

Sister Club: Brisbane Lions
Web Address: www.lions.com.au

Santa Cruz Roos

Santa Cruz Roos Australian Football Club
431 Del Mar Avenue
Pacifica, CA 94044

Web Address: www.santacruzroos.com
email: exec@santacruzroos.com

Sister Club: Kangaroos
Web Address: www.ozemail.com.au/%7elkatz

Seattle Cats

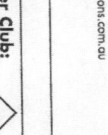

Seattle Cats
23833 21st Drive SE
Bothell, WA 98021

Web Address: www.seattlefooty.com
email: jim@seattlefooty.com

Sister Club: Geelong Cats
Web Address: www.gfc.com.au

TABLE 2-3
USAFL CLUB WEBSITE DIRECTORY

Atlanta Kookaburras	www.atlantafooty.com
Baltimore/Washington Eagles	www.baltimoredceagles.com
Boston Demons	www.bostondemons.org
Buffalo (Under Development)	www.usfooty.com
Chicago Swans	www.chicagoswans.com
Chicago Sharks	www.chicagosharks.com
Cincinnati Dockers	www.cincinnatidockers.com
Dallas Magpies	www.usfooty.com
Denver Bulldogs	www.denverbulldogs.com
Detroit Overdrive	www.detroitfootyclub.com
Florida (Under Development)	www.usfooty.com
Illinois Ironmen	www.usfooty.com
Inland Empire Eagles	www.eaglesfooty.com
Kansas City Power	www.kcpower.com
Lehigh Valley Crows	www.lvcrocs.com
Los Angeles Crows	www.lacrows.com
Louisville Cats	www.usfooty.com
Milwaukee Bombers	www.milwaukeebombers.com
Minnesota Freeze (Under Development)	www.usfooty.com
Nashville Kangaroos	www.nashvillekangaroos.org
New York Magpies	www.nyfooty.com
North Carolina Tigers	www.nctigers.com
Orange County Bombers	www.ocbombers.com
Philadelphia Crows	http://phillycrows.homestead.com
Phoenix Scorpions	www.phoenixscorpions.com
Portland/Oregon (Under Development)	www.usfooty.com
San Diego Lions	www.sandiegolions.com
San Antonio (Under Development)	www.usfooty.com
Santa Cruz Roos	www.santacruzroos.com
Seattle Cats	www.seattlefooty.com
South Carolina Hawks	http://members.home.com/rodders/schawks/index.htm
St. Louis Blues	www.bluesfooty.com
Tri Cities Saints	www.usfooty.com

TABLE 2-4
USfooty WEBSITE STATISTICS FOR 2000

Website Statistics

Timeframe	October 1, 1999- September 30, 2000
Number of Hits for Home Page	51,456
Number of Successful Hits for Entire Site	2,568,141
Number of Page Views (Impressions)	624,506
Number of User Sessions	136,400
Average Number of Hits Per Day	7,017
Average Number of User Sessions Per Day	373
Average User Session Length	00.08.06
Number of Unique Users	23,315
Number of Users Who Visited Once	18,018
Number of Users Who Visited More than Once	5,297

General Statistics

Players Registered on website (July-Oct)	728
Tipping Competition Entrants	2,651
USfooty.com web mailing listees	190
Junior USfooty Kick Packs sold from Website	22

TABLE 2-5
USAFL INCOME STATEMENT
(1/1/2000 to 12/31/2000 - on a Cash Basis)

INCOME

USfootyKick	$ 1,214.00
AFL grant income	66,575.00
Commission	1,370.11
Foreign exchange gain	1,881.49
Interest Income	62.80
Revolution merchandise	1,9015.00
Sponsorship Income	11,224.35
Advertising	750.00
Club dues	6,600.00
TOTAL INCOME	91,592.75

EXPENSES

Bank Charges	133.71
Conference Call	2,249.79
Insurance	1,700.00
Legal fees and consulting	3,750.00
Club development	2,657.04
Junior development	2,774.70
Printing & stationery	792.50
Public relations	7,741.33
Medical supplies	45.64
National game	4,042.02
Net national tourn. Expenses	6,470.88
Merchandise	7, 259.06
Reimbursement	542.40
Website	1,399.54
Telegroup dividends	330.50
Telephone	359.19
Trademark registration	410.00
Umpire development	3,263.92
Administrative/office supplies	870.51
TOTAL EXPENSES	$ 46,792.73

NET SURPLUS   **$ 44,800.02**

TABLE 2-5

USAFL INCOME STATEMENT (Continued)

Reconciliation of Net Income to Cash on Hand
Cash as of 13/31/99	$ 13,812.90
Add: YTD Net Income/(loss)	44,800.02
Cash as of 12/31/00	$ 58,612.92

USAFL BALANCE SHEET

(As of 12/31/2000)

ASSETS

Cash - Bank of America Checking	$ 11,173.89
Cash - Bank of America Savings	935.07
Cash - Members Credit Union	46,503.96
TOTAL ASSETS	**$ 58,612.92**
MEMBER FUNDS	**$58,612.92**

Buffalo, another fledgling team, was just beginning. The enthusiasm at this important conference was infectious, exuding confidence for this new United States Sporting Chum. The national championships were first held in Cincinnati in 1997 and again in 1998 and 1999. Santa Fe Springs, Los Angeles, hosted the Championships of 2000 with Washington/ Baltimore accounting for 2001. The Tournament moved back to the Midwest in 2002 with Kansas City, one of the founding clubs, hosting the championships. It is to the credit of these four venues that excellent and uninterrupted, if exhausting, football was held. Two adjoining fields were found for each tournament and much initiative was displayed. In Cincinnati the grounds were literally carved out of the forest. In Los Angeles, the second field was reclaimed from softball and baseball diamonds and in Maryland the two grounds were traced in the center of the Rosecroft Raceway. Although some variations in surfaces occurred, the Championships were held under safe and accommodating circumstances. Each team was accorded a tent for R&R (rest and recuperation), refreshments were served, USAFL paraphernalia and gear were available and although short in number, and frequented in even greater number, there were mobile pissaphones. In the case of Cincinnati, an obliging forest provided sanctuary. Ample supplies of water complemented the food supplies which ranged from traditional meat pies to the much broader menu of the Outback Steakhouse Restaurateurs. Each team played two or three games on the Saturday and the two championship contenders played three on the Sunday. Team numbers for the championships were limited to 16 players per team and each game consisted of two, 20-minute halves. Certain restrictions were placed after 1998 on the numbers of Australians who could be on the field at any time. In 1999 this proportion was 25%, in 2000 it rose to 40% and in 2001 it was pegged at 50%. Although this restriction impeded some clubs, most welcomed the philosophy and adhered strictly to these numbers. Umpires for each game were appointed by the USAFL and carried out their responsibilities assiduously.

The Championship results were as follows:
1997 Cincinnati defeated a combined team from Louisville and Nashville.
1998 Boston defeated Santa Cruz (easily)
1999 Boston defeated Santa Cruz (in overtime)
2000 Denver defeated San Diego (by 2 points)
2001 San Diego defeated Boston (easily)
2002 Denver defeated San Diego (easily)

Two of these games were so close that attending crowds rejoiced nervously and in the others the quality of football displayed by the winners, was hailed universally. The Boston Demons team of 1998 and the San Diego team of 2001 were superior to other winners, with combinations certainly approaching the standard of A Grade competition in Victoria.

The quality of the umpiring (center, sideline and goal) improved exponentially each year. In 1999 and 2000, the AFL rewarded one of its Grand Final umpires with a trip to the USA and a whistle to blow at the Championship games. Unfortunately, the events of September 11, in the

USA so disrupted air travel that AFL personnel were not in attendance at the Championships of 2001.

The Championships, however, provided opportunity for the clubs to meet, so the first Annual General Meeting was held in Cincinnati during the 1998 Championships, with 15 registered teams in attendance. This meeting followed the official formation of the USAFA in 1997 when the original eight clubs formed USfooty. A board was formed with duties dispensed to various members. Table 2-6 details the board members for the year 1999 and their respective duties.

TABLE 2-6
USAFL BOARD MEMBERS FOR 1999

Richard Mann - President
Chris Olson and Bill Dusting, VP – West
Tim Powell, VP – Central
Michael Giabardo, VP – East
Cameron Murray, Treasurer
Sheri Archer, Secretary
Paul O'Keeffe, Member-at-Large
Matt Muller, Webmaster
Wendell Stephenson, AFL Liaison
Mike Gardiner, Public Relations
Jeff Norris and Jim Baldwin, Junior Development
Jim Bradley, Umpire Development
Steve Arnott, Umpire Coach
Gary Hill, National Coach
Pam Kellett, Ex-Officio Marketing

Junior development has been high on the list of priorities from Day One. Jeff Norris from Chicago initiated this effort back in the early '90s. Paul Roos, veteran AFL champion, had a major impact in 1999 when he traveled the country giving clinics to juniors and coaching the seniors. An ongoing presence from the AFL continues to boost the USAFL's image. AFL umpires, Hayden Kennedy and Mark McKenzie, and finally, Ross Smith, the Head of Development from the AFL, Brownlow medalist and former St. Kilda champion, have visited the U.S.A. in various capacities.

Dr. Smith was especially praising of the junior development efforts under the current directors, Jim Baldwin and Greg Everett...

A final note of evidence for the success of the establishment of USfooty is the story of the national team that has played in four competitions to this date. The first was a game, held in Chicago, against Canada in 1999. The American Revolution ran out winners, 10 goals, 15 behinds (75 points) to 8 goals, 7 behinds (55 points). The team was honored to be coached by Paul Roos, a 356 AFL gamer. Paul started his coaching career in style by leading the Revolution in a hard-fought match in excellent conditions.

In 2000 the conditions were not as friendly when the Revolution traveled north of the border to take on the Canadians in the return rubber. This game resulted in another win for the US with 4 goals 17 behinds (41 points) to 2 goals 4 behinds (16 points). This game was played in Toronto on 30 July 2000. This time the team was led by newly appointed coach, Dr. Gary Hill. The third competition was a round robin for the Alliance Cup. Five countries assembled in London in early October 2001 to contest this trophy. Teams from Denmark, England, Ireland, Canada and the USA comprised the entries. Although the US team lost to Denmark and Ireland, they finished second in the overall accounting to the team from the Emerald Isle. It was not easy to select the teams as the clubs are so dispersed throughout the States, but a selection committee eventually performed this task with apparent success. The mitigating condition was exemplary. The team was, in modern terms, "State of Origin", in nature. All players had to come from US backgrounds or affiliations and Australians were prohibited. The fourth team to represent the US took part in the International Cup held in Melbourne in August 2002. This is discussed more fully in Chapter 7.

A committee developed to give Australian Football a mission statement in the United States confirmed the successful beginning. The statement read as follows:

> **US Footy Mission Statement**
>
> We are an amateur sports organization dedicated to the development of Australian football. We seek to accomplish this through keeping the code in the United States, facilitating the growth and stability of footy clubs in the United States, and by setting standards by which member clubs agree to abide.
>
> We are a grassroots organization which promotes participation in Australian football through promoting awareness and knowledge of Australian culture, by promoting a sense of community among USAFL clubs and club members, and by fostering junior programs across the United States and promoting extensive involvement in the game to non-players.
>
> We are the sole representative of Australian football for the U.S.A. in the international arena.

All statistics in this Chapter refer to the situation at the beginning of the 2000 year. It is difficult to keep up with all the momenta in such a fast growing enterprise.

The early cynicism concerning the success of establishing Australian Football in the USA has been placed well to the rear of the back burner. Frankly, today, it is thriving as the reader will see from the chapters that follow.

THE STORY OF USfooty

Chapter 3

THOSE RESPONSIBLE

The storied Australian poet, Banjo Paterson, would have written this chapter, probably in verse form, much better than the two authors of this story. For Banjo Paterson wrote about Australian characters from the bush with a special charm. The two main pioneers of the modern Australian Football in the United States more resemble Australian bush characters than they do the liberal set, the academic strutters or the modern sports administrators. Paul O'Keeffe is known as the founding president and Richard Mann has just finished a two-year stint as President of the USAFL. Of course, there are other characters who have contributed to the modern era and they shall be referred to, in due course – Sheri Archer, wife of Richard Mann and Greg Everett, current youth director, are two important pioneers also. Paul Whiting, who stepped up to work with O'Keeffe in1998, was the man who labored hard and long to consolidate the Boston Demons while, at the same time, fulfilling the onerous tasks of National Secretary. The presidential line of Paul O'Keeffe and Richard Mann was due salute to the expatriate factor – they were Aussies interested in transplanting a sacred piece of Australia in the US. In the spirit of developing and Americanizing the game, it is interesting to note that the presidential successor to Richard is the immediate past president of the Boston Demons, who is very American and eager to see the game established. His name is Jon Lenicheck and his vocation is administrator for a House of Representatives member from the Boston area, called Representative Michael Capuano.

PAUL O'KEEFFE, BETTER KNOWN AS 'PLUGGER'

Paul is Banjo Paterson's "man from the bush." He grew up in the outback of New South Wales in a mining town called Broken Hill. His Dad was the engineer of the main mine. Paul was the last of six children, but the long last by 17 years. By bush standards, the family was well educated. After a forgettable Primary experience in local State and Catholic schools, he moved to a high school in Queensland and studied for a Bachelor of Economics at the University of Queensland. He takes up the story: "My third calendar year at the University of Queensland was spent at the University of Massachusetts, Amherst, USA, on scholarship exchange." We conducted an extensive interview.

"By this time you were fascinated with the United States?"

"Yes and no. After an 'iffy' high school education, I went to the United States, which was fabulous. I only found out about the scholarship from an American, second hand. It was a secretive exchange, promoted circuitously because they only had three slots open and didn't want huge numbers applying. But I got in. I set my aims for a year, which consisted of 50 weekends with something to do on each. It was a party year, so I experienced an American College football game, a lot of caving in the Berkshires and skiing anywhere, it was a fabulous year. I spent a hundred days on the road and did ten thousand miles on Greyhound buses. Then I flew to London and tracked down Loch Ness in Scotland. Belfast and Dublin in Ireland were an essential side trip and a long trip back to the US Grand Canyon, eventually landing in Florida, finished a hundred-day odyssey before returning to U Mass. I wrote a diary every day, which detailed my economic capabilities. I averaged twenty dollars a day for one hundred days. This led to an economics degree. My return to Australia was not anywhere near as glamorous as the year abroad. In America, you network to get the right job. In Australia, you interview and keep your fingers crossed. I interviewed with AMP (Australian Mutual Provident Fund) in Brisbane and didn't get the job. The day after, however, AMP called and said,

'We have another job we would like to offer you.' and I asked in return 'When do I start?'

'Is next Monday OK?'

I am luckier, more than smarter than most of my colleagues, so I worked with AMP and the corporate world for the next two years."

When Plugger returned to Australia from the US, he naturally congregated with his former mates. Somehow, however, he found they did not have much in common so he struck out in different directions – the first was a foray into Team Handball which proved successful to the extent that in 1988 – 1989, he was selected in the Australian Team. This experience initiated him into sports administration. He became the Public Relations Officer of the Australian Handball Federation (AHF) and a board member of the Queensland Team Handball Association (QTHA). He put it this way:

> "My duties were a good combination for me, being a loser with no friends and no girlfriends. Indeed at this time no relationship with the opposite sex had lasted longer than five weeks, so I had time on my hands. I moved to Iceland to play Handball to find out how truly talented I was. I found that in Australia I was good, but in Iceland I sucked! And I was able to direct all my efforts to developmental work."

In Australia he ran foul of the imported European AHF President from Yugoslavia. While conceding that this coach was one of the best handball players in the world, as national coach and President he exerted vice-like control over his charges:

'I'm the national coach and when I say 'Jump", you jump!'

This confrontation was important for Plugger who felt that a coach had the right to ask players to jump, but felt that such an imperative must be accompanied by a good reason.

"Give me a good reason and I'll jump higher than any Yugoslav."

At this time, Plugger was 22 years of age and ready for travel. Through the handball network he contacted the President of the Icelandic Handball Federation who offered to help him find a team, accommodation and a job if he traveled to Iceland. Plugger added one more interesting piece of information:

> "My Mum, when I first went to U Mass, said 'Don't you marry an American', but she didn't say anything when I went to Iceland."

Plugger arrived in Iceland in January 1990. Things were desperate. He had no hotel, no money and had saved little, due to reimbursing his parents for his trip to USA. In Iceland in January its pitch black all the time, but he managed to spend a couple of weeks in a youth hostel. The Handball Association was ambitious. They were to attend Czechoslovakia for the world championships a month after his arrival. He organized a one-way ticket to Luxembourg, wangled the use of a car, and secured a press pass for the world championships. He found it unbelievable; he was walking with the world champions and experiencing delight at hobnobbing. He overcame his need to pay for a return ticket by traveling with the Icelandic National Team. He traveled with the national Icelandic coach whose name must be recorded, "Bogdan Slovanovich." The ensuing days were spent drinking, training, drinking and celebrating. The Handball crowd was an insular section of an insular society, practicing, mateship, and all of the other behaviors that go with a minority team in a general sports environment. Plugger didn't waste his time. He enrolled at the University of Iceland and worked for a local company. With characteristic frankness, he called himself at this time "a jock who wanted to pick up women in the bars in Iceland". Banjo Paterson would have loved writing about the predicament in which Plugger soon found himself. At the University of Iceland, he met a lovely American girl who was on a Fulbright scholarship who later became his wife. Their courtship is a story in itself. The academic coursework of his future wife, Julie, was complete and things were getting expensive. Fortunately she salvaged some monies from her Fulbright scholarship and was able to save enough money to fly the pair of them to England in the middle of the Iraq war.

"We spent the next two years in relative frustration. I wanted to play Handball for the Australian National Team in trials for the Barcelona Olympics in 1992. This did not work out. We eloped and married on 20th July, 1991, so I could get a green card and we could return to America. We traveled around Australia visiting my family. We even made it back to Broken Hill."

"Are you still married to this girl?"

"Unfortunately, we are now divorced. It had been touch and go and a few times we split up, only to get back together. I followed her career for the first five years after returning to the U.S. We lived in a small rural Midwestern town during that time. She worked for three years as a librarian at Monmouth College. I vacillated between desk top publishing, selling my mother-in-law's folk art, coaching soccer at Knox College and studying for an MBA at Western Illinois College. The emphasis of the degree was Entrepreneurship and Sports Management. After the degree we moved to Milwaukee where I was fortunate to land a job with Andersen Consulting (the firm has since been renamed Accenture")."

The seeds of his entrepreneurial future were sown at this time.

"We had a child called Heather and I pursued my team handball interests. It led to some basic preparation for the Olympics in Atlanta. I was the 'Field of Play Coordinator' for the 1996 Atlanta Olympics. It was one of the most amazing experiences of my life.

Like every Australian kid I grew up wanting to play in the Olympics. While I did not get to play, I still got in my Olympics in a capacity I am better at than being an athlete. This, ironically, was my last official involvement with handball. Little did I know it was about to be replaced with footy."

ENTER AUSTRALIAN FOOTBALL

When he was at the University of Queensland, he played one game with the university team's seconds, but had always liked the game, seeing it as part of the social fabric of Australia. Like so many pioneers, Plugger happened on the game whilst in the throes of bringing his general ambition to fruition. He had only seen three games of AFL Football in his life, which is understandable in a country town like Broken Hill. However, the culture of Broken Hill, even though existent in the heavy rugby state of New South Wales, was more geared to South Australia, where the predominant culture is Australia's original game. He got involved with the Handball presence in Atlanta, but today believes that footy is lucky it is not an Olympic sport. He firmly believes that the emphasis on winning Olympic gold is detrimental to the development of any game. At the age of 28 in late 1995, he experienced great frustration with handball tournaments in Oklahoma City as a precursor to the Atlanta Olympic competitions. His handball career finished when he was rebuffed by his old Yugoslav rival for the position of competition manager for the Sydney Olympics. In his Broken Hill days he played every sport that he could find. He began to develop heroes and models at this stage. One was Craig Johnson, the young soccer player who played for Liverpool in the English and European competitions. Another was Adair Ferguson, a sculler from the University of Queensland who won world recognition in rowing. She was a Human Movement student who tried every sport imaginable until she found she had the perfect body type for sculling. Within nine months she won the world championship in Europe.

"I modeled her search and tried everything including Australian Football. As I look at the players in America today, I realize I'm not as good as fellow pioneer Rich Mann or Dustin Jones from Lehigh, but somehow, that doesn't seem to matter – all sports are worth playing and Australian Football is a particularly interesting challenge.

The first meeting about Australian Football took place in Chicago in October of 1995. It was an informal meeting to talk about the future. John Harrell of Louisville organized the meeting. He traveled to Chicago. An American called Paul MacAveney, who lives in Milwaukee, had lived in Australia and was intrigued with the game. He made the trip to Chicago with me. Other characters who joined us were Geoff Norris, an elementary teacher from Chicago, and Gavin Coote, who was married to an American and still lives in Chicago. Lisa Albergo represented the newly formed organization called AFANA (Australian Football Association of North America). John's vision was for a Midwest semi-professional league. I felt it was too aggressive and the approach should be focused on more of a participatory, lightning tournament format.

I disappeared off the scene for the next 12 months. I again became involved when a young Aussie in Madison left a phone message for me mentioning that I ran the Milwaukee team. I was confused until I worked out my name was on the website. I checked out the website and found that a number of teams had been formed over the previous 12 months, in Louisville, Cincinnati, Indianapolis and Kansas City.

I was about to start a long-term project in Kansas City. Harley-Davidson, my long-time client, was building a new factory in Kansas City and I was to travel to Kansas City for 15-18 months. My click on the internet produced a name – Jason Eustice. We would fly down to Kansas City on a Monday night work until 6 pm Tuesdays, and then go and play footy and drink afterwards. Jason was an Australian from a very famous football family in Adelaide who brewed his own beer and vinted his own wine – his Uncle was one of South Australia's greatest players.

Jason was blue collar, working class and didn't have a lot of skills in creating a club but his sheer passion set the sport alight. He recruited Americans, contacted the AFL, strung Indianapolis, Louisville, Cincinnati and St. Louis together and finally organized a match against Canada in Toronto. Jim Cooper from Los Angeles started his own club in Southern California, the Los Angeles Crows.

Things were so disorganized that on our way to play a weekend game in Toronto one of the group mistakenly made hotel reservations in a sex motel. It was hilarious when we closed the windows. There weren't any shades, only mirrors and we had difficulty extricating ourselves from the local traders to go training and to find a decent meal. I can remember this game well because within the first two minutes I was knocked over, winded and kicked a never to be repeated goal from the left pocket. My first kick in over ten years and it was a major."

He didn't think he would ever kick a ball again, but being an eternal optimist, he takes up the story:

"I thought I would die, but then I looked around at the guy that hit me and he was hobbling off. I had already kicked a miraculous goal and repeated this performance just before the end of the first quarter. We managed to stay ahead of Toronto for the rest of the game. We were hurting but we had a lot of fun."

Greg Everett from Toronto gave Paul a hard time because he insisted on calling this game "the first international game played on North American soil."

"We had representatives from Los Angeles, Cincinnati, Kansas City, New York and Milwaukee, so we felt justified in calling this a US team. We had some Americans like Ron Miller, who became a co-captain, so we were fulfilling the philosophy of Americanizing the game of Australian Football. This game, more than any other, was the birth of USfooty. Without this game bringing us all together the national body may never have been formed."

In August, in temperatures of 105 degrees, Kansas City and Cincinnati went to St Louis. Cincinnati picked up players from Louisville and Indianapolis on the way. Plugger made the trip down from Milwaukee.

"I will always remember that trip because about 20 miles outside Milwaukee the air conditioner packed up. It was a long trip with two small kids in the back."

Cincinnati lost that game, but later won the first National Championship in 1997 and can legitimately call itself "the first National Champions in the United States". In September 1997, Cincinnati held a tournament with six clubs in attendance - Los Angeles, Nashville, St. Louis, the Broadview Hawks from Toronto, a combined team from Kansas City and Louisville and the host-city comprised this first National Championship. Six teams played a round robin tournament and that night the USAFA was born. Although the venue was a forty-minute drive from Cincinnati, it was perfect. They found themselves standing on packed gravel in a tight circle, vowing to keep this game alive in this wonderful country forever. Rich Mann was there, so were other enthusiasts Geoff Cann, Gary Flesher, Mike Powers, Peter Beare, Gino (from Indianapolis), Jason Eustice, Jim Cooper, James Campbell and, of course, Plugger. Two other characters were present: Sam Ingram from St Louis and John Harrell from Louisville. Starting from this humble beginning, eight clubs were the founders. They were Washington, D.C., Indianapolis, Nashville, Louisville, Cincinnati, St. Louis, Kansas City and Los Angeles. Volunteers and clubs came out of the woodwork. One was Dean Thomas, who had started an umpire's association called AFUANA (Australian Football Umpires Association of North America). Dean offered to start the first website of the USAFA and he designed the first logo. The Umpires Association was given one vote on the new council. The initial approach called for each member team to run a tournament and there would be a season of football. Mike Powers, who was the founder of the Nashville club (and later the Atlanta Kookaburra's) became ad-hoc secretary, assembling the email addresses of the various clubs. Naturally, egos began to enter into this fascinating development. Jason Eustice and Jim Cooper verbally sparred with Plugger grabbing Jason's elbow on a few occasions to settle him down. It is to be expected that tensions would develop as the game's needs became evident and the passions of those involved reached breaking point. But the upshot of this first effort was that six founding teams came from the Midwest, with one from the west coast (Los Angeles) and one from the east coast (Washington, D.C.). It took some time for the egos to meld into a national association. Plugger takes up the story:

> "I was very strong about calling it the United States Australian Football Association (USAFA) because the whole concept of authenticity with the Americans was important. My vision was always to create an association as we are today, with juniors, coaching, umpires, developmental activities and ultimately, a national league. I also thought it was important to sell our philosophy of developing sport to the AFL. I spent a couple of months writing the first charter which, mercifully, is still reflected in the current constitution – it wasn't initially legal, but it attracted some very important new comers like Boston and Santa Cruz."

Plugger, in typical fashion, bashes all clubs equally. But he did admit that it was hard to get around the quick development that took place in Boston. He put it this way:

> "A close community with guys who wanted to practice the

eternal evidence of this wonderful game 'kick-to-kick' at every opportunity".

By early 1998 there were five teams in California and eighteen clubs in the states. Plugger requested US$5,000 from the AFL. He didn't ask for a lot of money for fear of refusal but, when he returned to Australia in January 1998, the AFL flew him to Melbourne from Brisbane for discussions. Characters like CEO, Wayne Jackson, Development Manager, Ed Biggs, and, of course, marketing guru, Grant Burgess, were there to meet him. He met with each of the AFL clubs and then, with two Boston stalwarts eventual president, Paul Clarke, and secretary, Paul Whiting. The other Boston club pioneer, Adam Mutton (Mutts), was there also. After a beer and a rousing session, they all agreed it was time for this wonderful game to take hold in the US. Some of the Australian clubs affiliated readily with the US enthusiasts, but some didn't. The LA Crows, for instance, never affiliated with the Adelaide Crows, but they were rare as the USAFA would not allow teams to affiliate with an AFL name without an AFL relationship, but in Los Angeles' case they were grandfathered in. There was some pettiness as US teams claimed their affiliations and it is interesting to note that the term "sister clubs" was preferred to "brother clubs" signaling willingness to depart from chauvinistic tendencies. One obvious combine was between St. Louis and Carlton. Who could deny the classic logic of "The St. Louis Blues"? Plugger's relationship and credibility with the AFL solidified. In his words:

> "They said they would pony up for $5,000 for 1998 and support us with a lot of equipment and junior footies."

Initially, O'Keeffe was the facilitator with the passion for putting charters together, getting philosophies in order, and keeping people on the straight and narrow. The AFL knew they were dealing with a dynamo, but Plugger realized he needed the status of officialdom to continue his negotiations with the AFL. He took the role of President of the USAFA in late 1997. He was careful to avoid egotistical claims and listened to the rank and file throughout his term as President. Plugger did understand the importance of branding. Maybe his tour of duty at Harley-Davidson had rubbed off, and he termed the name "USfooty." Surprisingly, the web site name was available so the site for this new game is "**USfooty.com.**" The ideal compromise had been struck, the official name USAFA anchored the initiative with its founding father – Australia, but the dynamics of USfooty brought the new chum into the trenches. There is some debate as to exactly when the Association was founded, but there is no doubt today that since early 1997 USAFA has been the effective voice of Australian Football in the United States. Today it is called the USAFL. The beginnings of ESPN cable television's coverage of the AFL "Match of the Day" introduced the game to sport America and began promoting the game with the American public. The Grand Final has always been shown live, even in 1997 when a group of Southern Californian businessmen arranged by special satellite coverage as none of the cable channels would carry the game. The other problem was that the finals when carried live would begin at 1 am and the pubs would close at 2 am. In 1998 ESPN2 carried the footage but were inundated with many letters of disgust when the TV station delayed the Grand Final for four hours due to a baseball match. ESPN lost footy in 1999. It was then that Fox Sports World began coverage. Plugger pulls no punches when he talks of the coverage being restricted to Fox Sports World and not on Fox Sports Net:

"The year 2000 sucked and 2001 sucked too".

He believed the USAFL was doing a lot of free advertising for the Fox Sports network, One interested character, Rob DeSantos, the founder of AFANA, tried hard to close the gap between the association and Fox, but failing health and the break up of his marriage sabotaged his efforts. Plugger realized that this game would spread quickly if regular television coverage were available throughout the states.

Other interesting developments at the time are worth noting. The International Australian Football Council (IAFC) had been founded a little earlier so the USAFL decided to pay their $50.00 for membership with this group. They had a web site with some interesting information on earlier history, especially World War II. Another ensemble, the Arafura Games, set up in the Northern Territory with football as one of its 20 sports. Apparently they held competitions in Darwin every other year. The name Arafura is taken from the Arafura Sea, which is the body of water just to the north of Darwin. Many local countries sent teams to this competition with Papua New Guinea defeating New Zealand in the most recent competition. The IAFC soiled their own linen by claiming that the AFL didn't really promote football internationally and that they were the true pioneers of the international game. This prompted the AFL to respond by telling them that they were not the games keepers and that they were out of line. Plugger decided to deal directly with the AFL himself and this was a shrewd and successful decision. Unlike any other world organizations, the AFL is both the premier league and the leader of the international support series. They have superseded all of the former associations and leagues around Australia and are in a prime position to push the game worldwide. But he also realized that Australian football was bigger even than the AFL. This has led to some interesting decisions in relationship to equipment and commercial support. There are some, too, he concedes, who are not sure if the AFL is really interested in promoting the game worldwide. He does not belong to this band of cynics pointing to the international competition under AFL sponsorship, which took place in Melbourne in August of 2002. Although the initiating sponsorships would undoubtedly arise from AFL sources, it was important for the new chums to begin traditions that would guarantee football's continuance around the world. He was particularly keen on the Atlantic Alliance Cup between Britain, Ireland, Denmark, Canada and the US, which began its tournament in 2001. O'Keeffe can take credit for helping to marshal the kind of effort that comes from trench promotion. Another question arose about the likelihood of recruiting for the Australian League Clubs. Did the AFL promote international football so they could encourage more swelling of the home ranks with outstanding talent from overseas? The example of Jim Stynes, the indefatigable Irishman recruited to Melbourne by Ron Barassi, and rewarding his efforts by winning a Brownlow Medal, is a classic instance of this development. Plugger realized that these isolated instances were going to happen but it was not a sustainable strategy to grow the game. The potential, however, of football following the cricket model, of having international visits with test series does have its own attractive promises.

Several other developments have taken place; an International Advisory Committee to the AFL was formed with seven people constituting its membership. Plugger's suggestion that three of these consist of one representative from Asia, North America and Europe has come to fruition. Ross Smith, Ed Biggs, and Peter Hanlon were joined by a character from Canberra representing the Jim Stynes Cup (a junior international cup) to make up the rest of the seven. Plugger suggested that perhaps credible Australian football greats like Paul Roos or Kevin Sheedy might make excellent committee members also. The point of the Committee is, of course, that it is only an advisory committee with accordingly proportionate and limited muscle. Plugger readily acknowledges that reams of correspondence and other communications must take place for an international association to function smoothly. He is quick to acknowledge the work of Rich Mann, Sheri Archer and Greg Everett. He is apologetic for the slow growth of his own club, Milwaukee, reasoning that this is due mainly to his preoccupation with national administration, but then is less perturbed when the overall viewpoint is considered. One does not need to belong in the company of US football leaders to detect a tension between Plugger and the two characters running the Nashville club. They spar constantly but the authors must confess that after a healthy exchange both Nashville combatants will turn around and wink at those behind them, unrepentant but distinctly mischievous. In the early days, Americans were part of the executive that helped Plugger in his negotiations with the AFL. Mike Powers from Atlanta, an American, was the first secretary and Elizabeth Ballagh, from the Tri-City area in Tennessee, was the first treasurer and opened the first bank account. She was an American married to an Australian guy who apparently was an excellent player for Tennessee.

In the critical years of 1998 and 1999, Plugger traveled to many US cities, visiting groups of enthusiasts who were starting up Australian Football clubs – Boston, Baltimore, and Philadelphia were three important recruiting areas. He is proud that by the end of 2001 there were 33 clubs in America and ten more with whom he was talking. Not all of these clubs were formed by expatriate Australians. He was proud also of the great story with a photo that appeared on the front page of the Australian Financial Review. This feature started with the question "How serious was Australia's brain drain and where did all the talent disappear?" This photograph pictured the Boston Demons, 1998 National Champions, with a biography attached to each member of the team. Only one was without an important University degree and he was a gas attendant from a local petrol station. Four of the team members were brilliant researchers from Harvard working at the cutting edge of investigation into Alzheimer's disease. Two were professors from local universities. Eight were Ph.D. students at MIT. The rest were ambitious and successful young executives in American business enterprises. It was an impressive display that surprised many Australians and delighted the board of the USAFL and the Boston Demons. (Page 188, 189)

Plugger speaks of the years 1998 and 1999 with special pride, it was an explosive year with tremendous growth and by late 1999 the operative word for the USAFL was "stable." Some disturbing things happened which he regrets. The international brewing giant with automatic Australian connections, Fosters, facilitated their support. They eventually lost to the South Australian brewing company, Coopers, who were very keen to take up the vacant sponsorship. There was some loose information, too, that Australian football was a rough game in the minds of the American mother. Constantly, US football was criticized for brutality and injuries. Indeed many a US child more resembles a pretzel than a human being by the time he reaches 14 years of age. Was Australian football to have the same effect or was it to be more like soccer, which won favor with the American mother for its skill, continuous action and absence of crippling injury. Plugger's board acted quickly. They insisted that the "kicking in danger" rule be implemented religiously by the umpires and the "shirt front" was outlawed. One of the authors was horrified at this development having been brought up in the wet, muddy puddles of Melbourne in an Australian winter and having picked himself up from shirt fronts several times each game. Yet on reflection that same co-author realized today that the shirt front, although crowd pleasing, is not necessary for our great game. So if the decision was to be made between pacifying the American mother and satisfying an unnecessary Australian tradition, then the result was obvious – goodbye Mr. Shirtfront. Plugger was also very aware that the Australian culture favored the fast play on style of a game like Australian football. He queried whether nonstop games like Soccer and Basketball were really popular in the American culture. After all, Baseball and Gridiron were incredibly popular and they could only be described as 'stop-start' sporting phenomena. A little thinking, however, about the co-existence of cricket and football in Australia made Plugger confident that similar cultural proceedings could be obtained in the United States. After 1998, some concern was expressed over the location of future National Championships. Wherever cricket is played, Australian football can follow easily for the oval shaped ground is too large for most American play areas. California and Washington/Baltimore were able to fit the bill, but areas beyond those two would have to be thoroughly researched. Boston, for instance, was keen to run the Nationals, but has only just found a satisfactory venue in the Boston area. The presence of stronger and weaker teams presented a challenge for the organization of the National Championships. This question also concerned the seasonal competitions throughout the year. It is amazing, however, how these things work out eventually. The stronger clubs tended to seek each other out and the weaker ones enjoyed their game for different reasons. Plugger is critical of the 1998 Boston team. He says they had but one goal, to win the National Championships. He is right. They arrived on Friday night and observed a 10 p.m. curfew. On Saturday night, they went to the dinner but drank lemonade. On Sunday they wiped the competition by many goals. This created, according to Plugger, great resentment because the team had performed with Olympian discipline and not joined in the recreational participation that was observed by all the other teams.

> "Boston was a great team, but they lost sight of the greater goal of building a fledgling sport and culture. All the other clubs hated Boston, not because they were good but because they were elitist. They could have enjoyed the camaraderie and still have pissed it in. They were good. It has taken three to four years for Boston to be accepted by the other clubs as mates."

Plugger is wrong here. When you create a serious competition, you expect serious involvement. Boston went on to win the next championship in overtime and then lost the next two due to fielding a team that was much less elitist. It's true that elite squads are hated, feared and resented, but those of us who have played on elite squads, like Essendon, Carlton, Melbourne and Hawthorn, know well the feelings of the dedicated life. Plugger needs to realize that the culture of competition does not rely only upon beer and meat pies. The authors would like to differ with Plugger on his conclusion that Boston did harm to the American development by being so strong. Perhaps Boston brought the competition to maturity and the excellence, with which Denver and San Diego followed in 2000 and 2001, respectively, could well attest to this conclusion. Plugger did concede that each of the Boston players, individually, was a very pleasant and friendly individual, so perhaps this is what one must take from this discussion. The falling out with Nashville continued in 1999 and 2000 with various shifts on matters of the constitution, the web site, and the interaction with the work of the individual clubs. Quite naturally, a spirit of 'west against the rest' with a lot of unfortunate and unnecessary paranoia developed during this time but individuals were more responsible for this development than teams. When the teams did get together either for social or competitive reasons little parochial hatreds or behavioral problems occurred. At the end of 1998, Plugger talked to Wayne Jackson in Australia and asked for US$40,000 support in the New Year. They advanced AUS$25,000, which although considerably less, probably reflected an appropriate amount at that time. One very complimentary statement that can be made about Paul O'Keeffe is his preparedness to air the dirty laundry. He wanted people to know "the good, the bad and the ugly" but was happy to say that the good outweighed the bad on most occasions. He takes up his point with precision:

> "We were not perfect. I said this to Paul Roos early 1999 when he got involved. I want you to report to the people in Australia that

we have our foibles like all growing children. Our strength has been that we have been able to hurdle these problems with the help of key people. We had the problem of Boston predominance in 1998. In early 2000 Denver went to Kansas City and defeated them 200 points to 1. The back room and chat room exchanges after that performance between Football America and Denver were disturbing. I was concerned that the AFL would disavow our association after these rows."

Plugger's reasoning that the Denver/Kansas City debacle is interesting. He reckons he doesn't want to play on a team that wins by 200 points, nor does he want to play on a team that loses by 200 points. His suggestion, which has been adopted throughout the country, is as follows.

"Play a half, then split the squads evenly and play a second half with much more competitive alignments."

A number of times in the next few years, teams would turn up for competition with less than the required number of players. On every occasion the home team has supplied the makeup numbers and, in some cases, permitted their better players to go across, making the competition stiffer and frankly better to enjoy.

In May of 1999, the USAFL ran an umpire's clinic in Denver. It was run by Max Whitman who was a good umpire working in Chicago for two years. It was attended by Paul Roos and Steve Arnott, Wayne Pollock, Bert Heymanson and Plugger. The clinic was a great success, helping the league to upgrade the vital position of umpire and setting up a tradition that would enable national and international traditions to develop. Unfortunately, Denver did not attend, but this apparent apathy was reversed in the months that followed. In 2000, the league ran an umpire's clinic the equivalent of level 1 standard obtained in Australia. In 2001 and AFL level 1 umpire and coaching clinic was added to this development with the AFL sending their staff to run the clinics. Every club in the United States applauded this initiative. The decision to involve Paul Roos was particularly gratifying as he has the personality and the background to be an excellent model of the great Australian game. The AFL supported these efforts with a US$10,000 grant that was enough to run five clinics. Roos eventually became a strong supporter of the USAFL both publicly and privately on his return to Australia. Roosy was the American Revolution coach in 1999, and lead the Americans to victory over Canada.

This experience and his travels to teams across the U.S. convinced Paul Roos that the U.S. experiment was both worthy and in need of support.

> "The machinations of 1998 and 1999 led to some important leveling of my behavior and that of those around me. Paul Whiting, for instance, would disagree with me as did others, and I would respond with appreciation rather than anger. I get headstrong, too, so I need guys like him on the board to balance me out."

Plugger didn't stand for president at the end of 1999 but supported Rich Mann who eventually became a very popular leader. He had some personal problems and decided that it was time for someone else with fresh ideas to lead the group. Plugger had a good relationship with Rich and soon to be secretary, Sheri Archer, so things continued without interruption. They got a new grant from the AFL and continued the incredible and rapid development of the USAFL.

Cincinnati once again organized the 1999 Championships splendidly with Boston again defeating Santa Cruz in the final. There were two divisions this year with fourteen teams. It all worked out well. The AGM was smooth with only minor differences occurring. They experienced all the difficulties of a new and ambitious organization when dealing with the commercial world. The hotel they originally agreed to rent for all teams in the Championships told them they were two minutes from the field but in the end they were 30 minutes from the field, so they pulled out and ended up in the Marriot. The original hotel threatened to sue them for $12,000 in lost revenue. Characteristically, Plugger reported this as "God got us out of that, somehow." They asked the Australians for US$100,000 in 2000 and the AFL came back with AUS$125,000. They did not complain. They did want the Americans to use only AFL sponsors but they could not agree, especially as they had had a brewery sponsor on Plugger's desk for $25,000.

> "Fortunately, I didn't have to deal with Fosters because they didn't want to speak to me. The airlines presented another difficulty with sponsorship. We were supposed to go with Ansett and not United Airlines, and Air New Zealand was not interested."

The brouhaha was not necessary for both Ansett before it stopped operations altogether and United were members of the Star Alliance and therefore working members of the same family. Their liability discussions were problematic, but this ended up in agreement as people backed down from their original positions. Plugger spent $20,000 on postage, telephones, printing and other things at that time, including floating the Nationals in 2000. He didn't get much money until finally $120,000 was deposited in Australian dollars in their Australian bank account. They lost traction in the changeover from Ben Buckley to Ross Smith in the AFL. A lot of time was spent in negotiations but they were happy that Ross seemed to be the first guy in the AFL that was actually thinking about the international future of the game. Their efforts were attracting Australian attention and although matters stalled after the September 11 tragedy in New York, the priorities and the direction remained strong. One concern was that in the East Coast cities there were no multiple teams. The design was to convince the Boston's, Chicago's, New York's, Nashville's and Denver's to create multiple teams within their own purviews. It was reasoned that with local competitions, more interested people would play the game and better representative teams would result for the cities. His feeling that the game would stagnate with just one team in large cities like Boston is perhaps dramatic and a little overplayed. It is better for teams to develop at the initiative of individuals rather than the designation of club boards. The presence of so many fine universities and private and public schools in a city like Boston is probably the direction in which the next few years should lead. The recreation departments of universities are always looking for new experiences and, provided there is a body of students eager to start a new sport, it will be facilitated. What is needed is the time investment of dedicated young men and women like those on the board of the USAFL. The authors have not the slightest doubt that this will develop in the coming years. Plugger is right, though, when he says the people in this growing sport right now are there for the love of the sport, not because they want fame or fortune. He is further accurate when he believes that Australian football when presented and promoted in the schools and with sporting clubs would spread like wildfire across the plains of Northern America. The current efforts in Phoenix exemplify this position. He is also wary about current USfooty cities developing professional teams. He believes that too much emphasis upon super leagues does not succeed without well established developmental feeder operations. As with most pioneers Plugger is concerned with succession. He believes succession has to be prepared and planned. He loves displaying the photo of all the players taking part in the National Championships in 1999. He has a huge photo hanging in his living room that is to his universal delight.

He says, "I am more proud of that photograph than any other. That photo sums up all the hard work over the formative years of the league. All that work, and success, is embodied in that one photo."

He was also pleased in 2001 at the special meeting in Cincinnati in April that a constitution was successfully voted upon. He had become aware that things needed to be done quickly and formally if they were to continue and solidify. Plugger O'Keeffe, a brilliant pioneer, persistent and dedicated, deserves the plaudits for being called the foundation president of Australian football in the United States. There is little doubt that his efforts have provided the impetus for the successful adventure. It must also be recorded that things have not been easy for Plugger as they are not for pioneers in almost every other enterprise in which humans indulge. He can rejoice in one great resolution that it is largely due to his efforts that the taking of Australian football to the United States is finally succeeding.

We have introduced Patersonian poems to salute our pioneers. Perhaps the following one does justice to Plugger.

"Ave USfooty"

By A. B. "Banjo" Paterson

Long ago the Gladiators,
When the call to combat came,
Marching past the massed spectators,
Hailed USfooty with acclaim!
Voices ringing with the fury
Of the strife so soon to be,
Cried, "*O Plugger, salutamus te!*"

Nowadays the massed spectators
See the unaccustomed sight --
USfooty gladiators
Marching to their last great fight;
Young and old, obscure and famous,
Hand to hand and knee to knee --
Hear the war-cry,
  "*Salutamus Plugger te!*"

Fight! Nor be the fight suspended
Till the corpses strew the plain.
Ere the grisly strife be ended

> Ten and eight must be slain.
> Slay and spare not, lest another
> Haply may discomfit thee:
> Brother now must war with brother --
>   Plugger *"Salutamus te!"*
>
> War-torn vet'ran, skilled debater,
> Trickster famed of bridge and road,
> Now for each grim gladiator
> Gapes Oblivion's drear abode.
> But Plugger's last great final jury
> Turn their thumbs up -- it must be!
> *"Ave, Plugger and USfooty, salutamus te!"*

The *Evening News*, 16 July 1904

RICHARD MANN

If Paul O'Keeffe was Banjo Paterson's "gladiator from the bush," Richard Mann is Banjo's "Bushman's Song."

> "I'm travellin' down the Castlereagh, and I'm a station hand,
> I'm handy with the ropin' pole, I'm handy with the brand
> And I can ride a rowdy colt, or swing the axe all day'
> But there's no demand for a station-hand along the Castlereagh
>
> So its shift, boys, shift, for there isn't the slightest doubt
> That we've got to make a shift to the stations further out
> With the pack-horse runnin' after, for he follows like a dog
> We must strike across the country at the old jig-jog"

Richard Mann is the great rover of USfooty. Not unlike Paterson's man from Castlereagh, Richard Mann has played for most US teams, traveled from city to city and has the distinction of losing to Denver four times in less than 24 hours. He achieved this impossible task by playing for Cincinnati, St Louis, Dallas and Kansas City in a tournament in Cincinnati in 1999. He learned from that experience. Like the old saying goes, "if you can't beat them, go and join them," so Richard played in the 2000 championship team that defeated San Diego in Los Angeles in October.

"I had, of course, played for other teams," he says with a shy smile, "I came over to Boston and played for Nashville in 1998. We got a thumping that time".

But Richard in his travels can claim that he has played for two national champions, Cincinnati and Denver, and has also been on a team, St Louis - who kicked one point against Kansas City in June of '99- and guess who kicked that point - Richard Mann. He also played for the dominant Kansas City, but admitted that he only kicked one goal when playing for this dominant team. But we are ahead of ourselves.

Richard Mann was born in Perth in Western Australia where he played his first football game with in the South Suburban League. He started with the juniors playing in an Under 8 side. Rich continued all the way through his teenage years in the same league. One brother was on the verge of going to the Senior State League and another brother, who was a tough guy, would have succeeded, but he was not really into football. His Dad is another story. He was an accountant who played senior Football with Claremont. He had the distinction of playing in the 1964 premiership team and was at St Kilda when they won their only premiership in 1966.

Richard, himself, qualified as a Physical Therapist at the end of 1992 from Curtin University. He worked for two years in a Western Australian hospital before he joined a recruitment company whose job it was to fill the huge shortage of health workers, nurses and physical therapists overseas. He moved to the US in 1995 enjoying "red carpet" treatment with the intention of working and remaining in the States. He started in Louisiana and worked for 18 months before he transferred to Florida. His work periods of 3 to 6 months were known as locums and he completed three of these before he moved to Tampa, Florida, and then back again to Louisiana for a fourth period. While visiting friends in Cincinnati in 1996, he trained and played in a scratch match against Louisville. He loved the camaraderie of the fellow pioneers, so he decided he wanted to become involved at the very beginning of USfooty.

"I arrived on a Wednesday, got in and before I unpacked, someone asked me if I was going to training. What do you meaning, training?"

"It's footy training , so come for a kick"

> "I went down, but didn't have any boots, just shorts and shoes. I then found that I was to take tonight's training session as the most experienced guy in the group. – and I loved working up a sweat. It was first kick to kick, and then a mini scrimmage, and finally a little later, it was a scratch match against Louisville."

He relocated to Cincinnati at the beginning of 1997 where, from the ground up, he became involved with playing, coaching and the organization of the club. His initiatives were rewarded as he became a member of the inaugural national champion team, Cincinnati, at the end of the summer of 1997. Rich was a "doer" and a "Belonger." He became regional vice president at the end of 1998, helped organize the national championships of that year and was "best on the ground" in the 1999 national team that defeated Canada. That same year, he helped organize the national championships for the third consecutive year where he had the good fortune of meeting and working with AFL veteran, Paul Roos.

Two guys who should also be considered pioneers, whom Richard met at that time, were Geoff Cann, from Cincinnati and John Harrell from Louisville. They had met each other through the net, so they became buddies and training partners. Rich Mann became friendly with both.

> "The game with Louisville made me realize how much I missed footy. Although I liked the USA lifestyle and knew I would stay longer in the country, the Cincinnati people made me feel at home. Jean Mangharan, her husband, Kevin Murray and the mercurial Geoff Cann were my original motivators. Cincinnati might have been the original team, certainly from the central American states, but other teams settled in as permanent combinations during the 1997 season – Nashville, Louisville and Washington who lost to us in the 1997 grand final, Kansas City, St Louis and Los Angeles numbered amongst these teams. The Broadview Hawks, who were a combined team from Canada, also sent a group to the '97 finals series."

Rich refers at this time to one of the great problems preventing the setting up of Australian Football in the United States – grounds of sufficient size to take two 18 member sides. He talks about a problem that all start-up clubs have faced:

> "We effectively drove the city and every green open area. Eventually we found twenty available sites before hitting the local councils for permission to set up shop."

"And the result?"

"We still cite that situation, yes, yes. During that year different games were played as far as Wellington and at a high school west of St Louis before we settled on a ground at the Wellington High School. We were assisted by Dr Murray and another guy called, Reuben Gordon, and I can remember snow flurries coming across the ground for our first game. Sporadically, during that year we tried to hold meetings and a couple of elections for we needed organization, money and leadership. We, of course, looked for pubs, played horseshoes and stood around chatting before finally forming a club."

And Rich Mann was a vital cog in the organization that unfolded around Cincinnati

Rich succeeded the inaugural president, Plugger O'Keeffe, at the elections for President in October 1999 and continued to hold this post for the next two years. His efforts undoubtedly helped solidify the Australian game in the U.S. Soon after assuming the national presidency, he moved to Denver and played in their 2000 championship team.

Rich Mann played in several games against Boston during the years '98 and '99. The Semi Finals in '98, when Boston beat Cincinnati, comfortably, saw the first loss in Cincinnati's club history. Rich Mann was extremely impressed with the expatriates from the New England area. He played for Nashville during the first game of '99, when they, with six players from Cincinnati and others, snuck home in the first game of the year against a depleted Boston team in what was, to that time, the best game of Australian football played on US soil.

The Annual General Meeting during the 1998 national championships keeps coming up, over and over, as the critical decision-making event in the stabilizing of Australian Football in the US.

AFL umpires, Hayden Kennedy in 1999 and Mark McKenzie in 2000 officiated in the championship games as the new century was heralded in, to the delight of all the clubs. Ross Smith, Manager of Game Development, attended, and U.S. Football rose quickly to the top of priorities with AFL CEO Wayne Jackson. Important changes occurred during Rich's period of responsibility. The national championships were relocated from Cincinnati to Los Angeles. Team recruitment continued voraciously and junior development was officially promoted through the naming of a national director, Jeff Norris, later Jim Baldwin from Denver, took over this position.

Funding from the AFL was greatly increased and umpiring through the aegis of two more clinics was greatly improved. Rich Mann, still relatively young, was included in the Atlantic Alliance Team in London and was an organizer for the international competition that played in Melbourne in August of 2002. When Paul Roos arrived to bolster national efforts in 1999, both Baldwin and Mann peppered him with questions, some serious, some not so. The serious questions related to the game's development in this new country and the trivial questions raised humorous replies:

> "What about Warrick Capper? Are those shorts of his really as tight as they appear?"

And,

> "Were you really lying on the ground when you took that mark against Fitzroy back in 1986?"

Roos was amazed

> "You know more about football than I do; I'm really impressed with the passion you show for this game of ours."

> "We pushed Ross Smith to come over for a week before the nationals to see some of our programs, especially an American coach teaching Aussie kids to play the game in Denver."

Mann's enthusiasm for football caused some reversals in his professional life.

> "Seriously I have regressed. I was a manager in a hospital department in charge of nearly 30 employees and moving ahead, but when I changed my location to play football, twice, I lost professional ground."

Mann continued his life story by admitting that there were two reasons for his moves – one was to the follow the football star and the other was his beautiful inspiration, a natty damsel called Sheri.

> "She started tagging along with me, then she took the lead. When I became National President, Sheri became the secretary."

> "Was she really interested in football?"

"She made the decision that if I was going to do this, she would do it with me. She had been in Cincinnati for about a month before the 1998 National Championships when I asked her if she minded standing behind the table, serving food and conducting all the menial tasks of supply. I hand-balled her a red hot potato and went off and played football. She performed perfectly and happily. In 1999 when it was obvious that we would have the nationals again, she took over the organization. She assured me that if I was going to be President, she wanted to be involved also, 'I don't want you sitting at the computer until midnight if I am not involved. I want us to share it'"

It is difficult for us not to appreciate Sheri as secretary. She has difficulty sitting for any length of time. Frequently she bounces to her feet, crouches next to people to inform them, organizes things, dispenses beer and wine cups and then sets off down the path with her shot gun heels -- tap, tap, tap, to keep the administrative wheels in motion.

Richard Mann rejoins, "And when it all settles down, we can hear her coming back tap, tap, tap and from the presidential chair you can see everybody sit up straight and pay attention."

"And in your experiences in Denver?"

"The '99 Denver team was an under achiever. We finished with 2 wins and 2 losses and frankly didn't try as much as we should have. I think we finished fifth in the nation that year. "

"That was a huge reality check?"

"That was the best thing that happened to us. We learned much, too, from Paul Roos and the Canadian game we played that year, but it was not until January 2000 that we reversed direction. My first day in Denver was in the middle of winter with patches of snow on the ground. I was wearing big ski gloves and felt that whereas Cincinnati was cold, Denver was bitter cold. But we busted ass, trained three times a week and started a running group. In the middle of 2000, we played Seattle and got thumped – but that was the only loss in 2000. Our team was very effective but, like all Australian football groups, any team can beat any team on a given day. It was in this year that Carlton beat Essendon in the penultimate game – nobody expected it, but it happened, sending Kevin Sheedy and his unhappy band, back to the drawing boards for the year 2000."

Denver was also unhappy because, in spite of many invitations to visit, only one club, Chicago, accepted. Denver has a beautiful ground, described as a "putting green" by some. But it is cold and is called "the mile high city", so altitude plays a negative part. Mann succeeded in convincing Ross Smith that much fertile investment territory existed in the U.S.A. It was almost destined that Ross Smith and Rich Mann would work well together. Apparently, when Smith was studying in Western Australia for his Masters Degree just after his St Kilda career had closed, he coached in the Perth League competition. Richard's father played with him for a few games. They were teammates. Rich takes up the story

"Talk about a small world. Who could have known that Ross, as a developmental officer, would later work with a teammate's son to create football miracles on the other side of the world?"

He met also with Wayne Jackson and Ben Buckley from the AFL. Rich Mann has a different way of dealing with people to Plugger and it is probably true to say that both have wonderful balancing skills when dealing with large institutions. His urbane approach ensured that he would be the first to learn from Ross Smith, incidentally, that the AFL proposition leapt from $30,000 to $125,000 in his first year of presidency. Indeed, they celebrated this performance in very typical fashion – Rich Mann had a couple of beers and Ross Smith had a couple of iced teas.

"You have done well, you must feel proud? "

"It is unbelievable. At the 1997 meeting, Plugger and I were sitting around having a couple of drinks and chatting. We hardly knew each other but, by the end of '98, we had become mates. We looked at each other intensely in the eyes and Plugger said 'Mate, this could go anywhere."

Rich Mann went on "We were not kidding ourselves. We were not prophesizing our own domed stadium in five years, or a professional league generating more money than in all of Australia combined, but we were suggesting, if quietly, that of the basic television cable channels, numbering six, it was a possibility that Australian football might become a flagship of one of these channels. There was still so much work to be done."

"How do you see yourself comparing with US Rugby? It has been around a long time, but one rarely hears about them?"

"Yes, they face similar challenges and will take years to mature, but I believe our game has the potential to excite more people more quickly than does rugby."

"Why?"

"Because of the involvement. Rugby is a head-on game, you are running at people expecting to be blocked or tackled. It is very like Grid-Iron. The awesome thing about Australian Football is that is a mixture of Basketball, Soccer, British Bulldogs and Keep-Away. It is a giant game with crowd-pleasing physicality."

SHERI ARCHER

Banjo Paterson fails me not again in his immortal poem, "Ambition and Art." The poem typifies Sheri with the first and last stanzas. It is with surprising ease that this great poet describes Sheri's contributions inimitably. When Sheri discovered that Rich was going to be at his computer until midnight, the description would go this way

> I wait for thee at the outer gate
> My love, mine only;
> Wherefore tarriest thou so late
> While I am lonely

She as the painter would be:

> So the painter fashions a picture strong
> That fadeth never,

And in our original Patersonian description of Rich as a Bush Song

> And the singer singeth a wond'rous song
> That lives forever.

The grant from the AFL requested the appointment of an executive officer. Sheri was promoted from seller of sandwiches and Secretary of the USAFL Board to Executive Officer in the short space of 18 months and she deserved every moment of this rapid promotion. She represented the backbone of the growing entities, - someone who worked tirelessly without remuneration for the sake of the general cause and assisted the decision-makers, specially her husband who was now chief. Her work in Los Angeles and at the Rosecroft Raceway in Washington, D.C., ensured smooth facilitation and cooperation with the local organizers. Her personality and fun-loving approach to life are very much part of the family that is now known as USfooty. Sheri and her husband, Rich Mann, returned to Australia for eight months in 2002 but Rich resurfaced for the International Cup series held in Melbourne in August of that year to resume their contributions.

GREG EVERETT

When discussing the true pioneers of the USAFL, the name Greg Everett kept springing up from several lips. He is a unique candidate for membership in the Pioneering Club because although an Australian, he resides in Canada and has been an important go between for Australian Football in Canada and the U.S.

In keeping with our Banjo Paterson theme we found a typical and appropriate selection.

The Geebung Polo Club
OR
"The Toronto Footy Club"

It was somewhere up the country, in a land of rock and scrub,
That they formed an institution called the Toronto Footy Club.
They were long and wiry natives from rugged Laurentian Side,
And the ball was never bounced that Torontans could not glide;
But their style of playing footy was irregular and rash -
They had mighty little science, but a mighty lot of dash:
And they played on snowy pastures and they were muscular and strong,
Though their gear was quite unpolished and their hairs and legs were strong.

And they used to train their players willing balls into the scrub:
They were demons, were the members of Toronto footy club.

Now my readers can imagine how the contest ebbed and flowed,
When Torontan boys got going it was time to clear the road;
And the game was so terrific that ere half the time was gone
A spectator's leg was broken – just from merely looking on.
For they waddied one another till the plain was strewn with dead,
While the score was kept so even that they neither got ahead.
And the Cuff and Collar Captain, when he tumbled off to die,
Was the last surviving player- so the game was called a tie.

Greg Everett is the kind of pioneer who needs the type of recognition that a Paterson delight guarantees. And, his background in Australian Football is strong. His grandfather was a valued member of the South Melbourne Football Club. His life membership with the Swans was passed on to his son and then to Greg. His grandfather was an assistant manager of the Victorian State Team in 1948 and 1950 and South Melbourne's delegate to the VFL. He played with the Reserves in the 20's and held many important administrative positions in Victorian Football. His father, Geoff Everett, was a founding member of the Narooma Football Club on the South coast of New South Wales. He is a life member of the Sapphire Coast League and a fan of Australian football in general. Young Greg played with Narooma on the south coast, and in '86 he played with the under-19 at East Lake in Canberra. He moved to England and played with the West London Football Club, which is probably the biggest footy establishment in Great Britain, and is today a life member of that Club. He has not stopped playing since 1983. He played with Narooma from '83-'90 in two positions, Full Back and Ruck. From '90-'94 he played with West London in England. In '94 he became General Manager for the British Australian Rules Football League (BARFL), which hosted the first International Football game between Britain and Denmark. On that occasion, the Brits beat the Danes by 93 points, which historians will note reversed the passages of history dramatically. Symptomatic of history, the Brits reverted to successive losses for the next seven years until their surprise victory in the Atlantic Alliance Cup in 2001. This British victory over Denmark enabled the United States to take second position, having themselves lost two games to Ireland and Denmark, but was able to derive percentage superiority over the Danes. He coached Great Britain in '93 and '94 on two Canadian tours before he moved to Canada in 1995. There he coached the Broadview

Hawks to runners-up in the Toronto League. He visited America for the first time in '98, bringing a composite team to play an equally composite United States team. In '99, he coached the Canadian team, which played the U.S. team for the first official International game in Chicago. He played and inspired the Lawrence Park Football team for six years, while administering the Ontario Australian Football League as President in 2002. In March of 2000, he made sure two friends drove to Raleigh-Durham in North Carolina to do a level 1 umpire's course. These two friends were Bruce Parker and a Matthew Glynn who is, today, associated with the Victorian Country Football League.

It is sad that the pioneers of Australian Football, Plugger O'Keeffe and Greg, Everett divorced their wives due to their total preoccupation with establishing Australian Football. Constant travel, internet preoccupation, time constraints and costs placed a strain on their personal lives that led to personal tragedy of divorce.

In 1989, the Canadian League began with two teams in Toronto and as of 2003 has ten. This predated the U.S. establishments by at least seven years. Greg is a visionary whose dedication has led him to some distinctive conclusions. First, he believes that all teams in the U.S. should establish junior development through metro leagues (9 or 11 a side) and through strong liaison with high schools. He recognizes that transient Australians don't help because they build quality and then disappear. Australian Football will "stick" only if sufficient Americans are recruited and trained in the skills of the game. He believes, too, in international competitions, pointing to the desperation which players show when they are likely to make that team. He is, of course, a great believer in the "State of Origin" principle. He also considers the role of junior strategy to be important, with clubs consisting of ministries and portfolios the likes of junior strategy. He also believes the USAFL and the CAFA will eventually merge and be administered by the North American Australian Football League (NAAFL). I guess in that time the U.S. Footy and Canadian Footy logos will also be merged. His personal life has changed also since November '99. He has become a Firefighter in Toronto. His influence in Football continues and he has continued playing, administering and umpiring in Canada. Between April 2001 and October 2002, Greg and another character, called Cameron Childs, introduced Australian Football to 17,000 schoolchildren. Greg is at the center of junior development and is pleased to report that Canada gets 15,000 Australian dollars from the Australian Football League for these programs.

There is little doubt that Greg Everett is an important pioneer in the development in U.S. Footy and Australian Footy.

PAUL WHITING

With apologies to Banjo Paterson.

I had written him a letter which I had for want of better
Knowledge, sent to where I met him down the Charles, four years ago,
He was counting when I knew him, so I sent the letter to him,
Just 'on spec', addressed as follows, 'Whitey of The Overflow'.
And an answer came directed in a writing unexpected,
(And I think the same was written with a thumb-nail dipped in tar)
"Twas his writing mate who wrote it, and *verbatim* I will quote it;
Whitey's gone to Boston droving, and we don't know where he are,'

In my wild erratic fancy visions come to me of Whitey
Gone a-droving 'down the Corrib where the Aussie drovers go;
As the stock are slowly stringing, Whitey rides behind them singing,
For the drover's life has pleasures that the townsfolk never know.

For Whitey is a dreamer whose nose is in the stars.
He thinks he comes from special stock; cockies and galahs,
He watches life so steady, as he scans the Sydney skies.
He stoops to save the wounded, from crocks and wretched flies.

He's fallen for an Irish lass, who wants him at her home.
Yet burdened by his Boston tasks till he is outright prone
But his greatest contribution which we never doubt one bit
Was to talk one pesky drover to become Coach Louttit.

For Darren wasn't sure he could weld a footy class.
He organized and fretted long to draw on motel glass,

But Whitey's toil produced an answer to all his dreams
And in return the Boston coach laid down his mighty teams.

> And the year before the century changed, great challenge to all did grow,
> The woes the new football league were primed to bring them low
> But Whitey stood by Plugger firm the game to help sustain
> And all the crocks arose with him USAFL to maintain.

Whitey so embodied the perspicacity of Clancy that we have taken terrible liberties to honor him and hope we will be forgiven.

Whitey was the worker; toil should have been his middle name. He sweated over the Aussie drovers in US land to help them become better students, administrators, footballers, professors and researchers. When Plugger was undecided as to stand for National President in 1998, he waited until he saw the Constitution of the National Board fearing his dominating presence might have caused division and brought about lack of progress. It was then that Whitey stepped forward and nominated for General Secretary because he knew he could work with Plugger having done so well in much earlier days with team handball. It was a selfless performance because Whitey knew the task of General Secretary to the Boston Demons would continue with greater burden and complication. Boston was about to lose most of its victorious 1998 team. This meant heavy recruitment and much more time investment from the secretary. Indeed only seven members of the 1998 Boston team were available for the 1999 Championship team. In the space of one year, expatriate mobility had threatened to devastate the team and indeed this was Boston's year of truth. Had they failed to muster the support the indigenous numbers and the original enthusiasm they may have folded at that time. The USAFL was ready to bounce forwards with a zeal that also demanded total dedication. The indefatigable Paul Whiting rode both tasks to perfection giving him an honored place in the pioneers of Australian football in the USA.

Plugger completed this important chapter on the Pioneers of USfooty when he published a list of original pioneers from each club.

USfooty Celebrates

This October USfooty celebrated its fifth anniversary. It has been an amazing journey. One in which we have made strides on a monthly basis and achieved some staggering milestones, such as the Revolution trip to Australia and over 230 games played in 2002 alone.

Many people have invested countless hours into the growth of the sport, at both the league and club level.

Given we are a club-based organization, this seemed an appropriate time to recognize those individuals that have founded the various clubs over the years. These people will be forever remembered as the pioneers of Aussie footy in America.

Many of the people listed have since returned to Australia, but we can celebrate the legacy they have left behind.

I hope that every USfooty player will seek out the founder of their club and give them a very personal "Thanks, mate," for without their foresight, energy, time, craziness, and commitment you would be playing this great sport.

And, a sincere thank you, from me. Without your efforts the league would not have flourished over the years.

Paul "Plugger" O'Keeffe - USAFL Founder

List of Original Pioneers for Each Club (Continued)

Founder	Club	Year Founded
Cameron Ashe	Baltimore/Washington Eagles	1998 USAFL Founding Club
Mike Powers	Atlanta Kookaburras	1998
Miles Simms	Austin Crows	2002
Paul Whiting	Boston Demons	1997
Paul Clark	Boston Demons	1997
Adam Mutton	Boston Demons	1997
Rob Burgess	Boston Demons	1997
John Roe II	Boston Demons	1997
Dean Jackman	Boston Demons	1997
Warrick Burgmann	Chicago Sharks	2001
Sean Quinn	Chicago Swans	1998
Geoff Cann	Cincinnati Dockers	1996 USAFL Founding Club
Kevin Murray	Cincinnati Dockers	1996 USAFL Founding Club
Brett Ryan	Dallas Magpies	1997
Andrew Holland	Dallas Magpies	1997
Chad Stover	Dallas Magpies	1997
Craig Jones	Denver Bulldogs	1998
Erik Bilicki	Detroit Overdrive	1999
David Martinez	Illinois Ironmen	2000
Jason Eustice	Kansas City Power	1996 USAFL Founding Club
Robert Giabardo	Lehigh Valley Crocodiles	1999
Jim Cooper	Los Angeles Crows	1996 USAFL Founding Club
John Harrell	Louisville Cats	1996 USAFL Founding Club

List of Original Pioneers for Each Club (Continued)

Founder	Club	Year Founded
Trevor Church	Louisville Cats	1996 USAFL Founding Club
Chris Parsley	Louisville Cats	1996 USAFL Founding Club
Paul O'Keeffe	Milwaukee Bombers	1998
Peter Beare	Nashville Kangaroos	1997 USAFL Founding Club
Marcus Dripps	Nashville Kangaroos	1997 USAFL Founding Club
Mike Powers	Nashville Kangaroos	1997 USAFL Founding Club
Erik Kalhovd	New York Magpies	1998
Seth McElvaney	North Carolina Tigers	1998
Wayne Pollock	Orange County Bombers	1998
Tim Ferris	Orange County Bombers	1998
Jeff Ward	Orange County Bombers	1998
Chris Hasson	Philadelphia Crows	1999
Andrew Lochhead	Philadelphia Crows	1999
Andrew Ashworth	Phoenix Scorpions	1999
David Haydon	Phoenix Scorpions	1999
Sam Conrad	Phoenix Scorpions	1999
Bill Dusting	San Diego Lions	1997
Paul Koch	San Diego Lions	1997
Wayne Callis	San Diego Lions	1997
Warrick Burgmann	Santa Cruz Roos	1996
Matt Muller	Seattle Cats	1998
Jim Trenerry	Seattle Cats	1998
Tony Maher	South Carolina Hawks	1999
Sam Ingram	St. Louis Blues	1997 USAFL Founding Club
Dave Nicholls	St. Louis Blues	1997 USAFL Founding Club
Warren Ballagh	Tri-Cities Saints	1998
Chris Adams	Vermont Eagles	2001

List of Original Pioneers for Each Club (Continued)

Founder	Club	Year Founded
Ryan LaPrade	Vermont Eagles	2001
Scott Strenski	Western PA Wallabies	2002
David Ulonska	Western PA Wallabies	2002

---

[1] All of the A. B. Paterson poems used in this Chapter have been released from copyright. In spite of this, we apologize to the Immortal "Banjo." Source www.uq.edu.au/~mlwham/banjo/index.html.

THE STORY OF USfooty

Chapter 4

FIVE CHAMPION TEAMS

Plugger O'Keeffe speaks of the importance of Australian Football imbuing the culture of the United States with the input of Australian Football. It is an ambitious dream but a necessary one. So many groups, cults, religions, and tribes have migrated to the United States in the last 400 years that the country's history reads like a Who's Who of world events. Some groups have arrived in anger, some have been thrown out of homelands and placed in refugee status, and some have migrated with the hope of improved living standards and greater wealth. Ellis Island in the shadow of the Statue of Liberty in New York has been the proving station for future US citizens. Many sporting groups have joined the cavalcade: Soccer, born in England and quickly spreading like wildfire throughout the rest of the civilized world, has struggled for a permanent place and looks like establishing greater hold with the women's version rather than the men's. Rugby was transported to the States early enough to resurface in the form of Gridiron football today. Rugby retains its own identity but is not a very important sport in the US. Cricket was popular at the turn of the 20th century but has faded to a few desultory Commonwealth teams in Philadelphia, New York and Boston. Ice Hockey has fared better, especially as so many northern champions have invaded from Canada and Europe. Baseball and Basketball are well established as is Tennis, Track and Field and Swimming. The Olympic sports have fared well, yet some are seriously struggling, men's field hockey for instance. Chapter 1 of this story details the difficulties encountered in transporting and establishing Australian Football into US Footy. It is evident that local teams with consistent competition and a well-ordered infrastructure would have to develop if Australian Football was to take hold in the United States. Since 1997, five teams have dominated this establishment with others following not far behind. Chapter 4 will deal with five teams who have seriously contested the National Championships since 1997. Cincinnati, although a non-event since 1997, has the honor of being the initial National Champions. Some people would argue that few teams existed to contest its hegemony, but this is unfair reasoning. Cincinnati started the ball rolling and deserved the credit for a succession of National Championships which has been both credible and fascinating. The Boston Demons arrived with a bang in 1998 and carried off the National Championships that year with one of the best-assembled teams ever to grace the playing fields of the States. The following year they scrambled home in a great game with Santa Cruz to win in overtime by six points. But the Boston Demons were Champions in 1998 and 1999. Santa Cruz is included in this chapter because it was runners up in 1998 and 1999. Its story is also classic. Denver enjoyed a superior year in 2000. It scrambled home against an unlucky San Diego that year by two points. San Diego avenged by sweeping Boston and the field aside on the Rosecroft Raceway in 2001. Its bustle and physicality upset a disappointing Boston on that occasion which finished runners up. Denver returned in 2002 to easily account for the opposition with a convincing victory. These clubs have featured strongly in the first six years of USfooty.

Cincinnati Dockers

Probably the founding father of the Cincinnati Dockers is Geoff Cann. Others quickly ranged along side him as the city became the meeting point. Rich Mann joined Cincinnati after playing the first game there against Louisville in 1996. It was in this fair city that the group of eight or ten stalwarts, the true pioneers, stood in a tight circle and vowed to create the Australian game in the US. Resulting from its 1997 National victory, Geoff Cann was voted MVP in the Championship game. This performance eventuated into the "Cann Medal" which is awarded to the best player in the Championship game each year.

Every time members from the Cincinnati team stopped in Melbourne they made contact with the AFL and the AFL clubs. It was Geoff Cann who contacted every AFL club for interest in sponsorship but none of them were interested except the Fremantle Dockers. It had just formed so the Dockers were interested in spreading the word. The name Cincinnati Dockers was born. By this time, Rich Mann's brother was playing with the original Dockers, the two of them melded into the football twilight with consummate ease. The Dockers' first loss was in the 1998 National Championship semifinal to Boston. Rich Mann played in that game and marveled at the strength of the New England team.

But Cincinnati back in 1996 was in a pioneering mode. Geoff Cann had met a guy called John Howell from Louisville, hence joint training. Another guy responsible for Cincinnati initiatives was Rubin Gordon. He is described as a "pretty bright kid" with lots of talk which naturally established him as a "net" type and it was through the internet that the contacts were first made.

Cincinnati was not always known as the Dockers. Indeed, for its first game with Louisville, known then as the Highlanders, the Dockers played as "The Tremor." It was in the next year, after establishing a sister club relationship with the Fremantle team, it became the Cincinnati Dockers.

After being knocked out of the 1998 series, the Dockers lined up for 1999. It began the year with a 6-point victory over the Boston Demons in Nashville - six excellent Dockers joined with Nashville on that occasion to bring about the first Boston defeat of its career. It was on the 27th of March, 1999. It played three more games against Nashville, Chicago and Louisville, winning all three before going down to Denver and St. Louis at Kansas City on the 19th of June. Performances were mixed from then on through September. The Dockers lost to Chicago twice, beat Milwaukee, North Carolina, Louisville and Nashville, but lost a big one on the 7th of August to Nashville in Tennessee. In the National tournament that year it finished third in their division with two wins and two losses. These wins, however, were important. It defeated San Diego on the first day and Missouri comfortably on the second day.

In the year 2000, Cincinnati recorded a record of eight wins and six losses. The Dockers got home by a point against Louisville in June but returned to beat the same club by 60 points two weeks later. It defeated Chicago and Milwaukee and accounted for Tri Cities and Illinois with comfort, but did not fare so well against Nashville, Boston, Atlanta and North Carolina. During the National tournament in Los Angeles, Cincinnati played poorly against San Diego, Chicago, New York and Phoenix. The 2001 schedule saw a record of 12 wins and 12 losses. It did register, however, a five-point win over a team not defeated before, Santa Cruz, in the National Tournament in Washington in October that year. In the 2001 USAFL Champions Cup in June, it defeated Denver by four points and lost to Boston in the final. Once again, the team fluctuated from month to month, reflecting a record of strong and weak teams depending upon the availability of players. In the 2002 schedule, it was to play important games against Boston, Denver and Santa Cruz in June. And scheduled on August 3rd was the Sixth Annual Cincinnati Cup involving Chicago, Illinois, Louisville and St. Louis. Another fine tradition which has arisen in this founding city is the Sixth Annual State of Origin match against the Louisville Cats on September 28th.

The Cincinnati rookie of the year, Jeremy Kraus, was selected by the USAFL to represent the States as the scholarship player of the year. He flew to Australia in April 2002 and trained with the Essendon Bombers for three weeks. It was the second year of this excellent program that had its inaugural selection of Justin Jones from Lehigh Valley. The 2002 Committee featured the names of none of the original pioneers which indicate Cincinnati's capacity to replace and continue strong administration with its pioneering team. The 2002 Committee was as follows: President, Todd McClamroch; Captain: Kyle Strenski; Secretary: Anthony Lewis; Treasurer, Bill Forsstrom; Public Relations, Tony Neary; Recruiting, Eric Merkie; Webmaster, Todd McLamroch.

The 2003 Committee changed a little: President, Todd McLamroch; Captain, Mike Hanavan; Secretary, Amber Gaylord; Treasurer, Bill Forsstrom; Public Relations, Jeremy Kraus; Recruiting, Tony Neary, who was also Metro League Coordinator; Social Club President, Erin Rothwell; Webmaster, Todd McLamroch.

To its credit, Cincinnati has continued to include Americans in its team rosters. In the year 2000, of the 25 players listed only three Australian citizens were included.

The Cincinnati Dockers were the first Australian Football Club organized in the United States. The Dockers formed in 1996. The first ever U.S. game was played in September, 1996, between the Louisville Highlanders and the Dockers playing as "The Tremor". Following a sister-club relationship with the AFL club, The Fremantle Dockers, they became the Cincinnati Dockers

Boston Demons

Although the official beginnings to this successful team are attributed to a fall afternoon in November, 1997, the real impetus occurred earlier. Paul Clark, Paul Whiting, and Adam Mutton sat together with Plugger in a Melbourne bar just after they had talked the Melbourne Demons into being their official sponsoring club. The Demons were singled out because the new club coach, Darren Louttit, had played a season with Melbourne in the mid 1980's. Someone had suggested that the Boston club was originally touted as the Boston Magpies. This is credible because the inaugural club president, Paul Clark, was a one-eyed Collingwood supporter. But this all changed and the Boston Demons club was formally founded in the Burren Pub in Somerville, Massachusetts, in November of 1997. The individuals present were Paul Whiting (Secretary), Paul Clark (President), Adam Mutton (Vice President), Rob Burgess (Treasurer), Dean Jackman (Web Master), and John Roe (Member at large). Their grinning faces can be seen in the club profile on the web site, ***www.bostondemons.org***. Soon thereafter Will Henwood (Marketing), Jane Hyland (Public Relations), Darren Louttit (Team Coach), and Member at large, John "Doc" Cheffers were added to the board. Liaison with the Australian New Zealand Business Council was enriched by the presence of Bill O'Connor who had played with the old Hawthorn team and who was a prominent hammer thrower in his native Melbourne. Tragically, he died in his sleep of heart failure during that first year. Coach Louttit dedicated the trophy to Bill O'Connor, a deed that was endorsed by the entire team. The other patron of the Boston Demons, "Doc" Cheffers tells the story of his inauguration:

> "I was sitting in the Hyatt Hotel, Boston, enjoying an Australia Day meal with Ranald McDonald (well known Melbourne journalist and former Collingwood President), wives and friends when suddenly the room was darkened. Six huge monsters hovered above me. What do you want? I tentatively asked."
>
> "We want you to join us in a wonderful adventure."
> "Who are you?"
> "We are the Boston Demons Football team"
> "I smiled. 'That's wonderful. Do you play games?'
> "We have our first game in April in Washington."
> "Oh? Do you train?"
> "Yes. Every Saturday morning at MIT."
> "Oh, even in the snow ?"

"Of course!"

So I went to watch this band of merry men run around MIT with their shorts on and snow flurries sweeping their hairy legs.

"How do you get over the fence?" I said.

"You jump the fence," was the enterprising answer.

I realized then that this training venue was very unofficial. Indeed this situation remained through March and early April in contest with women's rugby, junior baseball, and a hybrid brand of field hockey. But it was fun."

The Washington team sent a message to coach Louttit two weeks before their inaugural game. It said in effect

"We're pretty good. If you don't think you can hack it with us, we don't mind if you don't come."

Coach Louttit ordered training on a Thursday night as well in answer to this provocation.

The team assembled in Washington in a Hotel opposite the Australian Embassy three hours before the game. Players huddled in front of the bathroom mirror in Coach Louttit's suite. He had chalked his team on the looking glass in shaving foam adding last minute instructions to the backs, the forwards and those on the ball. We were ferried by obliging Washington personnel in their cars to the designated ground. The Cherry Blossom Festival had arrived first, so we drove further out. These grounds were occupied so we ventured further. Finally, a field was located which was suitable but in need of repair. A grandstand sat square in the middle of the field. Without a care, members of both teams lifted the grandstand to the side with little discomfort. Goal posts courtesy of Home Depot were implanted and Witches Hats designated the sidelines. Many diplomatic spectators assembled around the grandstand. "They look cute," was one Washington's supporter's evaluation of the Boston Demons. The umpire prepared to throw the ball in the air but before he performed this historic behavior, he was implored to replace his Washington's guernsey with a white shirt. Doc Cheffers looked at the Boston team and fretted. To a man, they were 20 pounds overweight but his concern quickly abated when he perused the opposition, to a man they were 40 pounds overweight. The first quarter saw torrid encroachments by each team with few scores, but soon thereafter the Boston team ascended and won the game comfortably. Both teams celebrated long into the night with the generous provision of VBs (the green Victorian Bitter beer can), the prized possession. Perhaps, mercifully or providentially, Australian ambassador, Andrew Peacock, was conspicuous by his absence.

The second game of that inaugural year was played against New York in the lower fields of Babson College, Boston. It was the first home game of this merry band. New York was now called the New York Magpies so a dour battle between the Boston Demons and the New York Magpies was assured. The lower end of the field was covered with water so the scoring end became the upper dryer end thus reducing the likelihood of heavy scoring at any time in the game. The Boston Demons convincingly won that game. It had three more victories against Nashville, and return games against Washington and New York on a Bronx field. By this time, Boston was seriously intent upon winning the National Championships in Cincinnati and achieved that goal with five more wins in the last weekend in August, 1998. Coach Louttit had forged one of the best combinations of Australian footballers this country had seen, then or now, and they were serious.

Nineteen ninety-nine was very different. The Demons lost all but seven of its Premiership side to attrition, graduation, visa expiration, spouse intervention (in the case of Slugger Slavin, fatal attraction) and the vicissitudes of the time. Coach Louttit expressed some doubts and Secretary Whitey desperately recruited amongst the wild Irish to gain the necessary numbers for a season of successful football. The result was an unrefulgent presentation of weaker and stronger teams. It entered the National Championships again scheduled for Cincinnati with a lower ranking than it truly represented. The Grand Final against its previous opponents, Santa Cruz, was a magnificent tussle. The Demons took its second championship by a solitary goal, kicked in over time.

A change in coach occurred for the next season with Scotty taking over from Darren Louttit. Scotty Nicholas had played well in the latter half of the 1999 season and had earned his merits with a fine game in the Grand Final. An injury early in the 2000 season limited his action as a player but his approach to the team and life, for that matter, was very different from his predecessor. Darren Louttit, God bless him, looked as though he was going to die if defeat loomed. He conveyed this desperation to his team members and they responded with sacrificial dedication. Scotty was anxious to develop a permanent assembly in Boston so he spent much time in recruiting Americans and in teaching his charges the schemes and tactics of the game. Although intent and serious about winning the championship again, none of the wild-eyed crisp of Darren Louttit ever surfaced in Scotty. His players loved him and he assumed full authority. It was a difficult position for him to inherit especially after he lost the first game to New York in Boston. He was not helped by the enthusiasm of one back man who punched out his opponent on the forward line in front of the umpire, not once, but twice in the last four minutes of the game. Boston, which was comfortably ahead by 10 points with 4 minutes to go, found itself down by 4 points as the siren sounded. Scotty struggled with few Australians and many newcomers for the rest of the season. The team did well to finish third in the National Championships in Los Angeles that year. Although defeated by San Diego in the semifinal, it was ahead at half time and only one goal down with 4 minutes to play. Then, the wheels fell off and the team succumbed to the disappointment of all members of that gallant team. Two thousand and one saw a season of 13 wins and one loss. A magnificent run was performed through the National Championships until the final game against San Diego. The wheels fell off Scotty's team again in the first three minutes of that game. The Boston team did not live up to its capabilities and surrendered disappointingly to a very strong San Diego combination. Still the Demons' performances in the four years of its existence have been highly commendable. Today, President, Jon Lenicheck, is the USAFL's President being the first American to be so honored. Fellow author, Greg Narleski, has assumed the Boston Presidency through 2002 and has become a keen devotee since he was a member of the 1999 Premiership ensemble. The Boston Demons team is proud of its Honor Roll that is recorded as follows:

BOSTON DEMONS ROLE OF HONOR

1997-1998 Boston Demons Club Board
President Paul Clark
Vice President, Adam Mutton
    Marketing
Public Relations, Will Henwood,
Secretary, Jane Hyland
Treasurer, Paul Whiting
Members at Large, Rob Burgess, John
    Roe II, John "Doc" Cheffers
Webmaster, Dean Jackman
Team Coach, Darren Louttit

1998 Boston Demons Club Board
President, James Thompson
Vice President, Adam Mutton
Marketing, Andrew Blencowe
Player Development, Tommy Ruyle
Secretary, Paul Whiting
Treasurer, Adrian Purtschert
Operations, Craig Atwood
Webmaster, Dean Jackman
Team Coach, Darren Louttit
Member at Large, John "Doc" Cheffers

1999 Boston Demons Club Board
President, James Thompson
Vice President, Adam Mutton
Marketing, Andrew Blencowe
Player Development, Tommy Ruyle
Secretary, Paul Whiting
Treasurer, Adrian Purtschert
Operations, Craig Atwood
Webmaster, Dean Jackman
Team Coach, Darren Louttit
Member at Large, John "Doc" Cheffers

2000 Boston Demons Club Board
President, Jon Lenicheck
Vice President, James Thompson
Marketing, Anthony Alembakis
Player Development, Tommy Ruyle
Secretary, Paul Whiting
Treasurer, Adrian Purtschert
Operations, Craig Atwood
Webmaster, Dean Jackman
Team Coach Scott Nicholas
Members at Large, Rob Moir, John
    "Doc" Cheffers

2001 Boston Demons Club Board
President, Jon Lenicheck
Vice President, Tom Ruyle
Marketing, Dean Jackman
Player Development Brad Rinklin
Secretary Steve Gain
Treasurer, Greg Narleski
Operations, Paddy Anderson
Webmaster, Dean Jackman
Team Coach, Scott Nicholas
Member at Large, John "Doc" Cheffers,
Suzanne Nicholas, Matt Barrett

2002 Boston Demons Club Board
President, Greg Narleski
Vice President, Brad Rinklin
Marketing & Communications, Will
    Skinner
Player Development, Chad Perkins
Secretary, Surf Del Mar
Treasurer, Beth Dressler
Football Operations, Heath McDaniel
Webmaster, Mark Freeman
Team Coach, Alan Nugent
Members at Large, Paddy Anderson,
    Alan Nugent, John "Doc" Cheffers

The 2003 club board was as follows:

President, Greg Narleski; Vice President, Jeff Tassi; Marketing, Will Skinner; Player Development, Jaime Gain; Secretary, Steve Gain; Jeremi Korpusik, Treasurer; Football Operations, Heath McDaniel; Webmaster, Brad Rinklin; Team Coach, Alan Nugent; Members at Large, Surf Del Mar, Melissa McConville; Jon Lenicheck. In 2002 extra positions were announced. Dean Jackman took over Hall of Fame, James Aylward became Demonologist Editor and held that position through 2003. He was also President of the New England Metro competition in 2003. Melissa McConville assisted with merchandise in 2002 and took on the committee to do with social activities in 2003. Jeff Tassi had charge of this committee in 2002.

The Demons have begun to propagate the game throughout New England. Each year it travels to the shores of Lake Winnepesaukee in New Hampshire to play a game against a developing team at a private college in New Hampshire. Faculty member, Doug Algate, is the pioneering force here and it is likely that a team will eventuate from this area. Another interesting development has occurred with the generosity and virility of Andrew Blencoe. Andrew rarely answers to this name preferring an alternative called "Psycho." Psycho has rearranged his backyard into a football field that is just under regulation size but large enough to play nines or elevens comfortably. The Demons have used this facility several times each season bringing Australian football to New Hampshire and combining it with an enjoyable social event. Psycho has also generously provided memorabilia and other Demon apparel for team use and for the Demons to sell. Psycho is a serious entrepreneur and challenged Scotty for the coaching position in 2002. The battle was royal yet it is fair to say the two are still good friends. Each summer the team trains with a graduate fitness class at Boston University. Many graduates from this institute have begun to sow the seeds of Australian Football in the Boston area. The continuing effort to involve Americans is well modeled by the naming of Heath McDaniel as team captain for 2001 and 2002. Boston sponsorship performances have varied in success but reflect enduring effort. The Overdraught on Cambridge Street in Somerville is the current watering hole. P. J. Ryan's Pub in the same town was the most recent watering hole. The Burren Pub and the Field Bars in Somerville and the downtown Times Pub were also prominent in earlier years. Melbourne Lord Mayor, Peter Costigan (a noted journalist), visited and enjoyed hospitality at P. J. Ryan's Pub in 2000. He generously donated 22 training jumpers on his return to Melbourne. Other donors include The Daylor Consulting group and Robert Half International Inc and Mark Skinner of Campus Group Holdings, Sydney.

Big changes were made in 2002. Scotty resigned as coach in January to take employment in the San Diego area. He kept an interest in his original team but checked out as so many ex-patriots do when employment opportunities knock heavily. He was replaced by Alan Nugent a champion player with the team since he was named best on the ground in the 1999 National Championship game. A heart and lung surgeon at Children's Hospital in Boston, Al Nugent has impressed everybody as a keen student of footy. He quickly had the Demons playing thinking football. The player response was excellent but team numbers had plummeted at the start of the season preventing the Demons from fielding consistently good teams. Also the newly formed North Eastern Division had excellent opposition with New York, Baltimore, Washington, Philadelphia, and Lehigh Valley leading the charge. The Boston team defeated New York for the inaugural premiership honors in September of 2002 but performed with uncharacteristic timidity in the national championship in Kansas City in October. Outstanding athletic trainer, Steve Budrick (also the Revolution trainer), remained steadfast in this post for all five years.

In keeping with the trend, Boston established a Metro League of four teams which played with between nine and eleven members in 2003. Consonant to and with the common trend, the names of four teams provided much fun. They were the Brookline Killer Bees, The Watertown Rats, The Jamaica Plain Buffaloes, and the Cambridge Lobstermen. Perhaps more important still, the philosophy of this league was simple -- "No one sits out."

Santa Cruz Roos

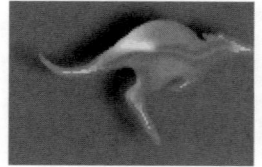

The reason we have included the Santa Cruz Roos in this chapter of the vintage US teams is because it has performed splendidly in two National Championships and three Californian finals. It was formed, like so many other teams, in late 1997 and grew to be a formidable team half way through 1998. It advanced to the finals of the National

Championships that year only to be swept aside by Boston in the championship game. The web reports for '99 signal much credit to the club. It is very tempting to say that the story of the Santa Cruz Roos centers on the presence of a giant of a man called John Ironmonger. He played in the AFL with distinction and comes from a renowned sporting family. His sister, Sally, was a brilliant member of the Australian Institute of Sport's Netball team and later represented her country with distinction. However, John, himself, would agree with Neil Radshaw, who maintains that the Santa Cruz Roos is a team and not a group of individuals playing the same game on the same field. He is proud of the manner in which his colleagues perform both on and off the field. Like so many others, the Roos has had difficulty securing grounds and has had to raise monies to hire those fields and to find insurance companies willing to guarantee the health of its players. The Roos say that its sponsorship efforts have had moderate success, yet its listing of supporters is beginning to look impressive. By 1999 the Roos had five strong backers: Brittania Arms Restaurant, Aptos, CA; Margaitaville, Capitola, CA; Australian American Chamber of Commerce, San Francisco, CA; Ocean Honda/Chevrolet, Santa Cruz, CA; Everlast of sporting and clothing sports good fame.

The team was unlucky to lose the 1999 National final to the Boston Demons when it battled to a draw at full time and lost the overtime play by just 6 points.

Junior Development Officer, Jeff Finsand, reports on commendable efforts to develop junior interest in the game. One game, for instance, called "Footy Nights," was played at the Walnut Heights Elementary School between 6:30 and 8pm on Mondays and throughout July 2001 this effort was repeated Wednesdays and Fridays. Efforts like these reflect the importance and wisdom of the name change to USfooty. It is of no consequence to youngsters whether the game began in Australia or not. "What they sees is what they wants." The nature of the game is sufficiently appealing to win youngsters' hearts and souls. The Santa Cruz Roos experienced a disappointing Nationals appearance in 2001 with air travel and other ventures interfered with by September 11th in New York. It was unable to muster its usually strong combination for these finals. At least many of its number were there and this is to their eternal credit. The Roos are sponsored by the old vintage North Melbourne AFL team. It has always had a fine connection with the Australian Football League. One the 7th of February, 2000, the entire football community in the United

States received a letter from AFL Chief Executive Office, Wayne Jackson, which was publicized through the Roos network. It read as follows:

"I would like to extend this word of thanks to all those people who have been and are involved in the building of Australian Football in the United States.

All the team at the AFL, have watched keenly the growth of the game during the last 2 to 3 years ago. I personally met with Paul O'Keeffe in December of 1997 as the USAFL was just getting underway. It is hard to believe that you are now up to 35 clubs and still growing.

Particularly, this message is to thank those people at the club level who have fueled the grassroots growth of Aussie Rules. For much of the time it is a thankless job and the glory is few and far between. But be assured, you are the glue that holds the structure together. It constantly surprises me the passion that Americans have for our great game and this gives much confidence for the future of the sport stateside.

We all hope very much you are able to keep up the good work. The AFL plans to continue to support you in your efforts through the national body.

Best of luck with the upcoming season.

Yours sincerely,

W.R. Jackson

Chief Executive Officer

Australian Football League

Melbourne

The Board Members for 2002 were as follows: Leigh Barnes (President); Rob Bell (Secretary/VP); Coach (John Ironmonger); Jeff Finsand (Development); Ryan Richardson (USAFL Delegate); Glen Gooding (Player Manager); John Ironmonger (Treasurer); Andrew Kramer (Grounds); Webmaster (Darrin Romasz).

The Roos were responsible for setting up their version of a Metro League which has become known as The Golden Gate Australian Football League. Particularly Junior Roos who are found in the elementary schools of Santa Cruz form clubs in this league called Marin, Oakland, San Francisco and San Jose. The driving force behind this initiative is old-time compatriot is Jeff Finsand.

The 2003 Board is headed by President Warwick Burgmann and USAFL Delegate, Neil Readshore.

Denver Bulldogs

Denver was formed in 1998 and their first real game was the ANZAC Cup in 1999 in Santa Cruz, California. As with most clubs matters started with a "kick-to-kick" in a local park. Its first competitive experience was played against the Denver Gaels Irish Football Club under the international rules adopted for such occasions. The Bulldogs won 61-44 points. Although formed in 1998, their first real game was the ANZAC Tournament on April 11th, 1999.

Armchair Aficionado, Jim Baldwin, plays with Denver. That is his American village. He talked of seeing this great game on the net and expressing great interest among his friends. But,

"We didn't have any players to play any games. We would read about it on the net, then go and have a beer with our mates to talk about it."

"The first team we played was Santa Cruz which was the number two team in the nation. We were the lowly Denver Bulldogs. Footscray had sent us size 12 woolen training jumpers, 1970's style, which were so tight that we were called strange names as we ran around the field. But they were red, white and blue and we wore them. Our chief, Jonesy, decided to get rugby shorts rather than footy shorts which are long and have flares and pockets in them. You can imagine my surprise when an unkind spectator called out 'faggot' I started out on the half-forward flank but I had no idea what I was doing so I decided to play ruck 'cos' ruck just follows the ball all over the field. The Santa Cruz dude who was guarding me was originally from Denver so we started talking. That's the great thing about footy, when the game lags you can chat with your opponent. We expected Santa Cruz to kill us but they only beat us 32 points to 14 and I kicked a goal and have a photograph to prove it. It's on my desk in the office and every time something goes wrong, I look at that photograph and say 'I can work magic also.' The story doesn't finish there. The goal umpire was my friend, Chris Olsen, and it was one of those broken plays where Jonesy at center half forward was flattened and fell on his face with the ball bouncing right to me. I turned and snapped it towards the goal. A guy dove in front of me and you could hear his fingertips touch the ball."

"You mean you didn't tell the umpire?"

"I'm yelling 'yah, goal' and it was a trifle funny because in the photograph you could see the opponent touching the ball. The umpire thought it was touched so he consulted Chris Olsen, the goal umpire, who admitted later that he felt sorry for us so he gave us the goal."

Jim Baldwin kicked three goals that weekend, all from the ruck. It was in April 1999 and he suggested sheepishly that the entire Denver team was playing in the ruck. That night everyone went off to the pub. He takes up the story.

"Now the ruck is a rough position. Your body is beat so I took a shower and stood in front of the mirror, naked, counting the bruises on my body. It was not a pretty sight. The guys were knocking on the door saying 'Jimbo, let's go - the beer is cold', and I can't even get off the toilet. I'm serious, I couldn't walk."

But later that night he confessed that the kicking of three real Aussie Rules goals was the apex of his career.

"I started on the back line the day the Canadians came to play. We were ready to have our backsides kicked so in a temperature of 96 degrees we challenged the Canadians who melt in circumstances like this. I played against a cranky old bearded Canadian who used invective with the same rate he guzzled water in the swollen sun. I kicked a goal in that game and am thrilled to say that my Mum and Dad were there. Dad was terminal with illness and it was the first and only time he saw me playing footy. He didn't know an Australian football from an Australian sausage but he had a great time. Thanks to Roosy and the unbleached sun we won the game."

Denver performed poorly at the National Championships but reversed this unwholesome performance the next year.

The year 1999 saw the Denver Bulldogs Football Club rise from obscurity to national recognition. In May of that same year, AFL legendary player, Paul Roos, visited Denver and conducted a coaching and umpiring clinic. Plugger was there with umpires, players and coaches from that region. By this time, enthusiasm and commitment were on the rise. A Kansas City tournament was a shining moment with Denver winning by a large margin. It had its first sobering moment in the finals that year in Cincinnati. Denver's performance was described as ordinary. But Denver was on its way. It was in serious search for sponsors and managed to get at least one of the local radio personalities interested in its efforts. In the year 2000, USAFL Rich Mann and his hardworking offsider, Sheri Archer, relocated to Denver. Jim Baldwin used the USfootyKick Program in his 4th, 5th and 6th grade curricula to promote USfooty. The National Association rewarded Jim by making him Junior Development Officer. The team finished the 2000 season with a magnificent win over San Diego in the Grand Final to become the third US club to win the national title. The Bulldogs were quick to honor the following founding members whom it credits as bringing the club from humble beginnings to the elite of the competition: President Matt Dainauski, Vice President Jim Baldwin, Secretary Paul Renouf, Treasurer Ian McNiece, Head Coach Russel Waugh; Webmaster Jonas Stoltz. Social Club Leader Sheri Archer was included in this group. Another creditable performance was the number of Americans playing in this premiership team. Of the 23 players on its roster, 14 were from the States. During that year Denver consolidated AFL relationships with the Western Bulldogs and affiliated with the Australian and New Zealand American Chamber of Commerce. As previously mentioned, Jim Baldwin introduced and directed his USfootyKick curriculum involving over 100 children. Ross Smith, AFL Director of Game Development, visited in October. In 2001 the players got their new guernseys from the Western Bulldogs. In April 2001, the Lazy Dog Pub agreed to sponsorship and that was the place for visitors to go to quaff ale when visiting the mile high city. The Dogs sponsored so many social activities in 2001 that it probably slowed them down for the Championship in Washington that year, but it is a fine combination. Its efforts in the finals of 2001 were commendable as it bowed out of the competition with a loss to San Diego in the semi finals. By easily winning in 2002 in Kansas City, Denver joined Boston as double winners of the national championships and reversed the results of the previous year against the San Diego Lions. The Bulldogs rue the fact that very few clubs visit them to play during each season. Altitude problems are, we are sure, the main reason. Notwithstanding the invitations continue to pour out from this adventurous and well-meaning organization.

It has full members who pay $60 annually and social members who pay $35 annually, and the fellowship engendered bodes well for the future of USfooty. The club officials for 2002 were as follows: Paul Renouf (President); Ben Harling (Vice President); Chris Candelaria (Secretary);

Ian McNieve (Treasurer); Tom Ellis and Destry Gillette (Sponsorship and Marketing Directors); Jim Baldwin (Junior Development); Glenn Rolfe (Social Club Director); Charles Richards (Coach); Ian McNiece and Matt Dainauski (Assistant Coaches).

Their guiding officials for 2003 are Glenn Rolfe (President); Aaron Beckett (Vice President); Dave Kennedy (Secretary); John Cudahy (Treasurer); Chris Candelaria (Sponsorship & Marketing Director); Tom Ellis (Junior Development Officer); Matthew Richards (Social Club Director); Charles Richards (Club Coach); Bruce Durrell (Assistant Coach).

San Diego Lions

National Champions
+ 2001

Big Bang Theory Revisited
("How We got Footy in San Diego")
By Bill Dusting

"When I arrived in San Diego in 1986, Aussie Rules was fading after its initial public frenzy. It had broken ESPN into higher ratings, and proven cable to be viable to a multitude of niche markets. The beach sports bars were packed with the curious, quaffing oceans of Fosters.

By the time I had a Sherrin sent over in 1989, ESPN had discarded footy, and Prime Ticket lacked the know-how to market and schedule footy, being more interested in full contact midget golf, and other such obscurities.

It was popular at picnics in the early 90's, thrilling drunken relatives and co-workers with my towering 25-meter punts. No one dared think about playing, as the TV marketing had portrayed the game as a free-for-all played by broken-nosed thugs, much like me.

I was happy in my sporting endeavors, winning obscure road races and triathlons that the talented overlooked, but my heart ached for the sport in which I laced a talent gene, footy. I was in college, May 1997 doing an internet course, and I punched up "Australian Football", on Yahoo.

My eyes were agog, as the primordial ooze of early seppo footy emerged. I read of games in the mid-west, but most importantly, a few hundred miles north were the Pasadena Crows. I rang Jim Cooper, the Crow President, and he suggested I form my own team. He armed me with the names of a few promising contacts.

Jon Yim, an American, who had been converted while serving in Exmouth, hooked me up with Paul Koch, an Aussie with an American boat-building business, Corsair Marine, who had at times traveled up to LA to Crow training with his sons, Neil and Evan. Jon put out a message on a primitive web-site, and the first training ever in San Diego was set-up.

I got in my early morning swim workout, and headed off to Balboa Park, expecting a plethora of footy heads. Alas, it was just Paul and I, but hey, a start. A few weeks later, Jon posted a training date for North County. Let me tell ya, I was very lonely by myself, and bummed at missing a long workout. I'd grabbed the mike at a 5k race I came second in. After prepping in the beer garden, my eloquent speech in front of 5000 attracted no interest. I let it go, convinced it wouldn't work. By a stroke of good fortune, I contracted pneumonia and other water-borne viruses during a race in polluted ocean water. I was hospitalized with a gammy lung, and while hallucinating with a temperature of 108F, and several pints of morphine, I dreamt that I could actually play and get the bloody ball rolling. It was at this time that Wayne Calliss called asking me if I wanted a kick and Jim Cooper was a continual pain in the ass, calling and cajoling, lest I stray. His Crows were stagnating, with no opposition for hundreds, nay thousands, of miles.

Around Grand Final time of that year, Wayne called to pontificate on his thoughts about the upcoming match-up between his Crows and my Saints. Needless to say, by the end of that game, I didn't like him very much. Contact was also established with the Down Under Bar's Steve Brownsea, with the hope that his establishment would prove a fertile recruiting den.

Paul Koch moved to San Diego permanently with his 2 boys in late 1997. By this stage Wayne and I were having a kick every few days. I harassed all my friends, but he just wanted to go surfing. My Minnesota mates, Joey and Jon Lethert on the other hand, were mildly curious, and completely drunk, and decided to come on out. I placed an ad in the San Diego Reader, that was completely ignored, and therefore 6 of us constituted the first training in February of 1998, at Standley Park. I had chosen Standley because it was near my home and work, and I was in a position of dictatorship.

Over the next few weeks, the likes of Mark Nichols, some Japanese exchange students, and Molly, showed up. The Koch's and I headed up to LA training in March. Afterwards, in a slice of hell Dante had looked over known as Aussie Bob's, Paul made the bold statement, 'Look, basically, let's just stop bloody screwin' around (pause to swallow another pint) and have a bloody game in 2 weeks in San Diego.'

After an introduction by Plugger O'Keeffe, Paul Koch successfully courted the Brisbane Lions into adopting us as their stateside sister team, supplying our uniform and identity.

The next day at San Diego training, there were 18 players, and we had our first 9-a-side scratch match. As I was doing the talking, I got voted the first San Diego President, with Paul as VP. Wayne was silently waiting in the wings, knowing that my manic zeal would cause me to implode in the very near future.

We searched high and low for a ground, always blocked by bureaucracy. With little time to spare, Paul got together with Paul O'Keeffe, materialized liability insurance, and enabled us to book a ground at UCSD.

At this point, I started to realize that club organization was a hotbed of frustration. As the game neared, the weak pulled out, and the meek deferred. On game day we had to press gang several who'd never even seen the game.

I was running around stealing witches hats from building sites, and using discarded piping for crude goals. On that historic April day, it was cold and rainy, and our bloody field was double-booked and swarming with pre-teen girls playing soccer. Thus, Pryatel did not host the first game, but Muir Field.

It got worse. The goal-posts collapsed and split Steve Brownsea's skull open and it started to hail. All the LA guys looked like they could play footy. A Kiwi, Dean Thomas, was umpiring. I started off at center half-forward, but my end of the ground was not required, as LA were busy with goal-kicking drills. In those days, they were a very formidable unit. Just before half-time, I managed to have a set shot from very close in, and kick our first point. In the last quarter we went wild, as Paul Koch snuck in our first goal.

Final scores   LA 24.11 155   SD 1.3 9

The score didn't matter; we'd created history by playing the first ever game of footy on the west coast of the USA. Pete Rowe of the San Diego Union Tribune wrote a story that was later repeated in the Melbourne Age, which brought about more players and more recognition. More games were organized against LA, including one in Riverside that caused the locals to form their own team. We traveled up to Santa Cruz, to play in the first Anzac Cup, and established ourselves as a superpower on the social scene, if not the field. Santa Cruz traveled down to crush us on our home soil, and to establish the Down Under Bar as the hotbed of post game merriment

. The CAFL came into being when Jon Egan, Jim Cooper, Paul Koch, Wayne Calliss, and myself traveled up to the home of Wayne Pollock to formalize footy in California. On my 38th birthday, the 2nd of August, the San Diego Lions won their first game, their first league game, ever, in defeating the Inland Empire Eagles. "Rooter", Darren Korn, was lured from LA with the promise of a job and cheap beer. LA was defeated in the 2nd round for the first time, as San Diego managed to put together a very formidable team.

However, inertia set in, and players disappeared into the hot Californian summer. Very few of those who remained trained, and I spat the dummy and quit. My ribs had been busted for the 2nd time, and it was no longer fun. This had the profound effect of strengthening the club under the new regime under the very able presidency of Paul Koch. Many of the regulars around the club today gelled into the type of cohesive unit at that time that made us an ongoing entity with a permanent future.

By then I was playing for the Orange County Bombers, but I watched with pride as San Diego salvaged the season, to just miss out on the finals.

I returned in 1999. In pre-season, we were getting up to 30 players at training, and were sophisticated enough to train under lights. More than half the team was American. Joe McAuliffe, though somewhat reluctant to take the mantle, was now Captain Coach. We were now well established enough to start accruing debt. The season started off disastrously, with the team unable to win. The highlight was hosting Santa Cruz in the very first night game ever played on American soil at UCSD. Howard Battye, Queensland's Super Rules State Coach, who was traveling through the States, saw us, and decided to stay. Joe gladly gave up the coaching, and the team became the stuff of legend. Cameron Trickey, a former Brisbane player, was recruited after he saw our huge 2-page spread in the local paper. We beat the unbeatable Santa Cruz on their turf, and proceeded to annihilate everything in sight.

We were proud to have Eric Aramian, and Jason Amstuz play for the US National side that defeated Canada. Training was near processional level in its intensity, and the players lapped it up. Come July, the club celebrated it's greatest day, by defeating Santa Cruz at the Rimac Arena, UCSD, by 2 points, to win the 2nd ever CAFL Grand Final, in probably the greatest game in American History. San Diego 6.8 44 Santa Cruz 6.6 42

The team could not rally to make its presence felt during the 1999 Nationals, having lost several players, and being burnt out by back-to-back CAFL seasons.

"It's now 2000. We've lost many players, but we can proudly say we've recruited more Americans to the game. Paul Koch has returned to Australia, and been made our first life member. Wayne Calliss has ascended the ranks to be CAFL President, and Eric Aramian, an American, is club President. We have a new coach, Chris Stiegler, who has AFL experience, and the future of the game looks healthy stateside."

Bill Dusting has introduced this club in what could only be described as delightful Australian linguistic flair. Like most serious ensembles, the San Diego group's fortunes fluctuate with the strength of its teams from week to week. Although winning the CAFL Grand Final in 1999, its performance at the Nationals in Cincinnati could only be described as ordinary. But 1999 was an important season. It had its first win of that season against the LA Crows and, a little later, gave Santa Cruz a big fight. Its new coach, Howard Battye of Coolangatta fame, improved the side by leaps and bounds. The team called itself a mixture of old and tired

Aussies with young and fit Americans. The effort in winning the CAFL Championship in 1999 was exemplary. In 2000 it installed Chris Stiegler as their new coach. He was a unique mixture of Australia and America, being a native of the US, born in San Jose, but having spent the bulk of his life playing football in Melbourne, Australia. He possessed a degree in Sports Administration and had played several games with the Reserves in the AFL. The Lions improved their performances dramatically with this new coach and repeated as CAFL Champions in 2001. In 2000 it defeated the Boston Demons in the semi-finals and went on to play a magnificent final against Denver in Los Angeles, losing by just two points. In 2001, in the shadows of the Rosecroft Raceway in Washington, it swept the field to win the championships easily. The San Diego Lions is supported by the Brisbane Lions in the AFL. The year 2001 was especially important to both clubs. Brisbane won its first AFL Premiership and San Diego its first USA Championship in that same year.

The Committee for 2002 was as follows: Michael Bailey (President); Lionel Benoit (Vice President); Wayne Calliss (Secretary); Rob Liwanag (Treasurer); Wayne Calliss (Manager); Justin McLarty (Social Coordinator).

The Committee for 2003 is as follows: Rob Liwanag (President); Mike Pekonen (Vice President); Jimmy Coyne (Treasurer); Ken Corlett (Secretary); Sharon Ferguson (Social Director); Mick Raher (Head Coach); Mark Taylor (Member at Large).

THE STORY OF USfooty

Chapter 5

THE WANNABE CHAMPIONS

At least 27 other clubs are in operation in the States today. The USAFL has established three regions that can be seen by perusing Table 2-1 in Chapter 2. There are some complications. Already in existence in the Western Zone is the California Australian Football League (CAFL) which runs its own competition, yet which does not include all of the teams in the Western zone. The CAFL has run its own competition since 1998 and consists of the following teams: San Diego Lions, The Orange County Bombers who absorbed the Inland Empire Eagles, the Santa Cruz Roos, The Phoenix Scorpions and the Los Angeles Crows. They function as a well-packaged league and hold as many as 19 games in the yearly schedule. Their latest official addition is the Phoenix Scorpions who joined in 1999 and who have already made great strides in developing junior leagues. Other teams reside in this region and play regular games against CAFL teams. The 2000 National Champion, the Denver Bulldogs, is one of these teams. Another important addition since 1999 is the Seattle Cats which has also made great strides as a football team and who are proving increasingly harder to beat as the new century develops. It was once called the Geelong Football Club at Seattle which was a bit of a mouthful so not surprisingly it is now known simply, The Seattle Cats. One more important beginner is situated in Portland in Oregon but has not made itself noticed as yet and is officially listed as under development. Centerpiece of the CAFL is the Los Angeles Football Club that has featured in developmental matters from the first days in 1997 through its redoubtable president, Jim Cooper. The Los Angeles Crows and The Orange County Bombers have enlisted the support of the Outback Steakhouse Restaurant group who has actually given their name to a Metropolitan Competition within the Los Angeles area. The enterprising names of these founding teams are worth stating: Westside Destroyers, Orange Crush, Valley Vipers, South Bay Sharks, Inland Empire Fire and South County Titans. Naturally, this metropolitan league, or "MetroFooty," is confident of becoming a force in USfooty. Their league coordinator, Craig James himself is a fireball and urges the football starved LA and Orange County public to come out and either play or at least watch the games.

The Central Region is a loose conglomerate of disparate teams some ragtag and some complete but all of them exude confidence and the type of enthusiasm that makes every game their last. Key amongst this group is the Cincinnati Dockers and the Nashville Kangaroos. The member clubs are as follows and they exist by playing round robin tournaments and grudge matches which are fast assuming legendary proportions: The Chicago Swans, The Chicago Sharks, The Kansas City Power, The Louisville Cats, The Milwaukee Bombers, The St. Louis Blues, and San Antonio, Detroit and Minnesota which are listed under development. One glance at the resourceful pen names indicates the presence of both Aussies and Americans with a keen sense of humor. Detroit, for instance, was not First, Second, Third or Fourth gear. It has skipped all those start-up moves and is now in overdrive and it continued as Detroit Overdrive for the 2002 season; however, it seems its speed in overdrive was such that its remaining players are now playing with the Chicago Swans. Another team that is under development is the Windsor Mariners which is just over the border in Canada from Detroit. This team began playing in the Ontario Australian Football League as part of the Canadian Australian Football Association. Such is the pace and versatility of start-up teams with resourceful personnel. Many of these clubs, too, date back to the beginnings of the modern era of USfooty and must be reckoned as having pioneer status.

The Eastern Region is a conglomerate of disparate ensembles, many of whom are already mired in "electric" tournaments. The Boston Demons and the New York Magpies are both tinder dry. The Tri-Saints team loses more games than it wins but it does so with great dignity. The Lehigh Valley Crocodiles is a bunch of high school youths melded together by the first coach of the New York Magpies who moved as a teacher into Lehigh Valley in 1999. It is an excellent, enthusiastic team of youngsters who have already made its presence known with surprise wins over more established teams like Boston and Baltimore/Washington. Several teams listed here are under development: Buffalo, Florida, and, until very recently, Philadelphia was found in this category. All teams listed have their web sites established with some in a state of flux accounting for shifting information from year to year but this is to be expected in these early years.

THE WESTERN REGION CLUBS

Two very successful clubs, San Diego and Santa Cruz, have been discussed in Chapter 4. The remaining clubs have interesting and unique features.

The Los Angeles Crows

It is important to list Committee Members and the various sub committees as these characters are responsible for the development of an important club. The General Committee is President, Jim Cooper; Vice President, John Pattison; Secretary, Craig James; Treasurer, John Stretton; Assistant Treasurer, Mike White; Club Captain, Jason Bottrell; Web Master, Darren Clifford.

This committee was supported by three sub committees. The first was called the Football Sub Committee whose members were as follows: Darren Clifford (Convener), Bill Lugg, Jim Cooper, Kevin Woolf, Chris Munz. This committee dealt with all the "nitty gritty" of preparing for scheduling, transport, and officials of the games. The Social and Marketing Sub Committee, whose members were Jason Bottrell (Convener), John Stretton, John Pattison, Matt Senko, Craig James, was responsible for the economic well-being of the club. Sponsorships, Publicity, Fundraising and Social Activities keep this committee busy. The third committee shows how important development and recruitment are to the Los Angeles Crows. Their members were: Justin Siebert (Convener), Jim Cooper, Robert Harrison, Bob Wagner, Mark Durston, Kevin Woolf. This Committee has created the Metropolitan League under the sponsorship of Outback Restaurants. It is this kind of activity that brings fiscal and expertise support from the Australian Football League in the Mother Country. In 2002 the new league began on the 19th of January. Round 1 saw the following games take place: South Bay Sharks vs. South County Titans, Westside Destroyers vs. Orange County Crush and Inland Empire Fire vs. the Valley Vipers. The web site of the Inland Empire Eagles notes that for the 2002 season it has temporarily downed their blue and gold guernseys and taken up the red, white and blue which is a symbol of a fire shield of firemen, and sponsors who are fully engulfed. They have rejected the concept of wearing Australian professional team uniforms and jazzed up a new uniform to meet the challenge of the new Metropolitan football league called the SoCal 9's. This new league has 9 instead of the traditional 18 players and is able, therefore, to compete on almost any ground in the United States.

The crows underwent an exhaustive 9-month planning in 1999. The team developed a strategic plan which followed a careful analysis of the Los Angeles basin area and Greater Los Angeles. It established a vision for growth and a mission statement with priorities, goals and objectives. Eight key areas were designated:
Coaching
Development of Australian Football
Marketing
Finance Management
Safety
Service
Operations
Facilities Development

The Crows believes it is in an unique position to establish a ready feeder for Australian Football to germinate in the States. It has attained non-profit status. It has a downtown Los Angeles corporate office on the 22nd floor of the Power-Com Building on 7th Street, just five minutes from the "Staple Center," which is home to the Los Angeles Kings (ice hockey), the Los Angeles Clippers, Sparks and Lakers Basketball teams, and the Avengers (arena football). The sponsorship drives have been very successful. Spicers Paper, the Horizontal Research Corporation, Show Film and the Australian Trade Commission in Los Angeles are the main sponsors. Marketing and Public Relations has been successful with an Australia Day Ball to honor <u>Fox Broadcasting</u>. The annual gum leaf award has been presented to David Hill and Jeffrey Rush, star of the film "Shine." And the Crows gave their shorts a baggier appearance in keeping with current demands for looser fitting uniforms. It has concentrated on a coaching development scheme and player skills development. In addition to rule modification, it has hired a Development Officer called Ross Dennis. Most of the Crows' home games are played under lights in the Sepul Veda Basin area and at the Woodley Cricket ovals. Players have seen the value of the co-existence of Australian Football and Cricket. Their team has benefited in performance strength due to its marketing and development programs. The program of establishing feeder clubs is proving helpful also. Five development regions were established by July 2000. They were Hawthorn (the Hawks), South Bay Saints, West Side Sharks, Pasadena Tigers and the Van Nuys Jets. A chat room has been developed where interested people can make contact and the 2002 season got under way on the 19th of January.

The Los Angeles Crows have created a stirring theme song. It goes as follows:

"We're the pride of California
The mighty L.A. Crows
We're courageous, stronger, and faster
And respected by our foes
Admiration of the nation
Our determination shows
We're the pride of California
We're the mighty L.A. Crows
We give our best from coast to coast
Where the story will be told
As we fight the rugged battles
The flag will be our goal
Our skill and nerve will see us through
Our commitment ever grows
We're the pride of California
We're the mighty LA Crows."

On the 19th of May, 2003, the Club lists the following office bearers: President, Chris Munz; Vice President, Bob Wagner; Treasurer, John Stretton; Assistant Treasurer, Mike White; Head Coach, Paul Scerri; Founder, Jim Cooper; Web Master, Bob Wagner.

Orange County Bombers

The Orange County Bombers team was born on July 19, 1998. In a sense, it was seeded by the Los Angeles Crows but, as it lived in Orange County and because there was a need for the southern Californian teams to form a competition, it broke away and became the fourth of the foundation teams in the USA's first league competition, the California Australian Football League (CAFL).

The Foundation members were James Campbell, Tim Ferris, Wayne Pollock and Jeff "Bomber" Ward. Orange County is the home of the Marine Corps Air Station known as El Toro. El Toro has been the home of

Marine Fighters for many years and is a key base in the strategic defense of the USA. The war movie "Independence Day" featured El Toro. The Bombers' inaugural captain, Jeff Ward, flew A-4M Skyhawks in the '80's as a captain in the Marine Squadron 311. This is impressive data when it is realized that the Skyhawks are better known as the world famous "Tomcats." This famous air station was also the home of the VMA-214 Blacksheep of "Baa-Baa Blacksheep" fame. For the same reason the Orange County Australian Football Club adopted the name of the Essendon Bombers. The selection of the team icon was more difficult. It decided on the name "The Bombers" because it contained personal touches of the founders and a successful Australian combination from Melbourne's North-Western section. It has fared reasonably well in competitions since. Its last game in 2001 was against San Diego in game three of the national tournament. Although losing 7 –7 (49 points) to 1-4 (10 points) it was far from disgraced. A full schedule for 2002 was planned with impressive social functions like: "The Rock'n Bowl" and the wine and cheese night at the Outback Steakhouse in Irvine sponsored by McPherson's wines who replicated this effort with the USAFL. Like so many other teams, the Orange County Bombers struggled to maintain recruits and a consequent standard of performance during the years 2000 and 2001. Training sessions would sometimes draw 17 members and sometimes only 4. After finishing the CAFL as premiers in 1998 and starting the next season well, summonsing as many as 25 players strong, it collapsed and slipped to sub par performance. Much of this was due to the return of Wayne Pollock to Australia robbing players of their main stalwart. Another reason why it has receded in current quality is the conscious decision to go with American players. This, of course, will bode them well in the years to come. The 2002 board reflected similar versatility as other clubs in that none of the founding members was a current member of the board: President, David Thurmond; Vice President, Simon Milburn; Secretary, Brian McDonnell; Treasurer, Scott Peters; Coach, Simon Milburn; Umpire Coordinator, Brian McDonnell; Junior Development Officer, Steve Cassity.

As of May 19th, 2003, the office bearers were as follows: David Thurmond (President), Chris Olson (Vice President), Brian McDonnell (Secretary), Scott Peters (Treasurer), Mark Seccull (Coach), Brian McDonnell (Umpire Coordinator), and Steve Cassidy (Junior Development).

The Inland Empire Eagles (now called Inland Empire Fire)

In May of 1997 the CAFL organized an exhibition match in Riverside, California. Three of the inaugural members of the Inland Empire team were at that match. The following weekend they got together for a kick and formed the Inland Eagles team. They eventually recruited a team of eighteen players. It was coached by a character called Jon Egan and played the Los Angeles Crows in its first game. It claims to be the first All-American footy team on the planet. The Eagles were beaten 156 points to 1 point and this drubbing seemed a disaster, but to coach Egan it was beautiful – he looked at the incredible potential. Not long after, articles appeared in <u>The Riverside Press</u>- <u>Enterprise</u> and the <u>San Bernardino Sun</u>. It was beaten by the San Diego Lions but experienced its first win against the Orange County Bombers. Seven straight wins saw them finishing on top of the CAFL ladder in 1998. The team has a strong junior development as many elementary schools in this region have taken up Australian Rules utilizing Auskick. The Eagles prides itself on their development of American players. This proved when Deron Lien and Brian Nickel were picked to play in the 1999 Revolution annual match against Canada.

The team experienced a metamorphosis in 2001. The identity was transformed from The Inland Empire Eagles into The Inland Empire Fire and began competing in the Nines competition within the Los Angeles sponsored metropolitan competition called the SoCal 9's. The ambition was to set California on fire with its colorful emblem and sensible transformation of team size to fit in with the smaller grounds in California. As outlined in the metropolitan league sponsored by the Los Angeles Crows, the business of the transformation from Eagles to Fire is explained. This remarkable performance indicates the flexibility and potential creativity of clubs in their founding years. It is a club that concentrates on Americans and is truly "state of origin." The willingness to change both philosophy and physical identity is a model which can be expected to be emulated in other parts of the States. It is very likely that a virile 9's competition will emerge under the auspices of USfooty that will rival rugby's highly successful 7's competition. Given the strength of the United States in world movements, it is entirely possible that Australian Football might be absorbed into the Olympic Games not as 18 or 16 men a side, but as the "Nines." As of the 19th May, however, the Club was still trading as the 18-men-a-side Inland Empire Eagles with Chris Olsen was

President; Brian Nickel was Vice President, and the delegate to the USAFL was Jon Egan.

The Phoenix Scorpions Now Trading as the Arizona Hawks

In August of 1999 a new club invaded the CAFL, not surprisingly the players called themselves "The Phoenix Scorpions." Its initiation was bathed in sweat and couched in sunburn for the few hardy souls who turned out for the initial training who found themselves in The Valley of the Sun where the temperature was 110 degrees. Since that time, its ranks have swelled and players' enthusiasm has grown in direct correlation with their drinking and cursing skills.

This Arizona club has shown remarkable initiative through its strong capacity for youth promotion and problem-solving ability. It has, for instance, developed Metrology (in conjunction with the USAFL) which consists of a zestful developmental concept involving youth, teams with nine players, league dues, social functions and the capacity to enmesh adults and youth in the same competitions. The assembled USAFL teams in Cincinnati in April of 2001 were mesmerized to hear John "Pops" Meier describe this concept in detail. It is an excellent model for developing USfooty. Meier is the Arizona Australian Football League (AZAFL) Commissioner. The Scorpions are the sole team in this state league – similar in nature to the CAFL, but have no intentions of remaining so. Interest has been expressed in the formation of a new club from Tucson where Anthony Starks is the initiating pioneer and even as far as San Antonio which envisages a team called "The San Antonio Diablos." USFooty is thriving in the desert areas close to where the recent Winter Olympics were held. Current office holders for the Phoenix Scorpions are: President/Treasurer, Andrew Ashforth; Vice President, David Haydon; Commissioner, John Meier; Director of Player Personnel/Coach, Sam Conrad; Junior Development Officer, Jeff Purcell; Marketing/Sponsorship, Matt Burke.

In 2003, the Scorpions took to the skies in the form of Hawks, deciding that the new club name, The Arizona Hawks, more embodied their increased horizons. Some changes in the Board occurred: Andrew Ashworth (President), David Haydon (Vice President); John Meier

(AZAFL Commissioner), Jeff Purcell (Director of Junior Development), Eric Aramian (Head Coach), Robert McCandless (Social Director), Stan Jones (Umpire Director), Sam Conrad (Player Personnel Director), David Pack (Managing Director), Brad Palumbo (Travel Coordinator), Jim Hill (Equipment Manager), David Marli (Webmaster).

Tucson Javelinas

True to their promise, the Arizona Football League materialized their interest in forming a new club in Tucson and they are known as the **TUCSON JAVELINAS**. They seem to be a bunch of interesting characters led by President Anthony "*Squirrel*" Starks, Vice President John "*Sweets*" Martinez, Treasurer-Coach Rob "*Blossom*" Massey, and Webmaster Gorge "*Pimp Daddy*" Pina. Breaking tradition here, the authors decided to include the team with their redoubtable nicknames: Neil "*DILF!!!!*" Dilts, Ryan "*Rhino*" Starks, Robert "*Mick*" McGill, Patrick "*Spongebob*" McLaughlin, Kevin "*Jeb*" Brown, Allen "*D&D*" Campbell, R. "*BOOOOOOOOONE!!!*" McLaughlin, George "*Chef*" Saliba, Toby "*Circle-K*", Bruce "*Airforce*" Noble, Donnie "*New Kid.*", Ernie "Dingo" Villa, Erik "Squid" " McCarren Grymko,

The Seattle nee Cats now Grizzlies

The driving force behind this growing club, whose enthusiasm and dedication will soon result in national prominence, is Matthew Muller. Matt has set out his club history in concise form.

> "Initially, the Seattle Football Club was formed on Grand Final Day 1998 (September) after a discussion between a few Australians who lived in Seattle and wanted to bring the excitement of Australian Rules Football to the Pacific Northwest. Over the following three months, the club recruited heavily, resulting in over 40 people on our member list. On December 13, 1998, after a short introduction for the uninitiated, the first game with seven players per side was played on a shortened field.

"After the Christmas break a social gathering was held where an official committee was elected and the Seattle Jets was decided upon as our team name. A second game was played in late February with eight new players deciding to pull on the boots.

"In mid March we changed our name to the "Geelong Football Club of Seattle," upon gaining sponsorship from the associated professional club located in Australia. A few weeks later, 13 players made the trip down to Santa Cruz for the Anzac Tournament to play our first games against other clubs. After winning our first two games and surprising a lot of people with our skill level, we were beaten by a slim margin in the championship game by last year's national runner-ups; all in all, a great performance for our first outing.

"After a short rest period we began training for the National Championships to be held in October in Cincinnati, Ohio. With 22 players and two coaching staff making the 2000-mile journey, we faired well against class competition. We missed out on a final berth by one game after losing to the eventual winners, Boston, ending the tournament with three wins and one loss, good enough for third in the country.

"Once again, during the off season we recruited hard especially for American players. In late April of 2000 we once again ventured down to Santa Cruz for their Anzac Tournament where we put on a strong showing with 30 players making the trip. Winning our first two games against nationally ranked Denver and Los Angeles, we faced Santa Cruz in the final, as was the case in 1999. Unfortunately, the result was the same as Santa Cruz ran out winners.

"In July 2000, we participated in the Bank of America Downunder tour in Seattle, showing approximately 250 school aged children about Australian football in short 10 minute sessions.

"In October of 2000 we once again participated in the National Championships in Los Angeles with a squad of 28 players and support staff making the trip. After a very strong showing in the round-robin games with a record 2-1, we came up against Boston. Although we were leading at half time, Boston managed to take victory in the quarter final game by 2 goals."

As with most teams emanating from Seattle, the cost of transport is at times prohibitive. This club enjoyed journeying to Santa Cruz because the transport was accessible. It is hoping Portland will develop as that journey is also well within the club purse. It needs sponsorship and has been busy developing this aspect of club life. A bottle shop, which sells Coopers beers, is one of their major sponsors. Sister club, Geelong, has also been helpful. It held a very successful Grand Final function and has posted entertaining photos on their web site. It has also experienced success in getting the Bank of America's Down Under Tour to give it a booth and an opportunity of promoting the game to school children. In July of 2002, it was looking to Vancouver in Canada to develop a team and providing competition. Bottle Works and the West Australian Football Group, Burley Sekem were also helpful for start-up operations. It made $1,500 from a Grand Final function at a venue not difficult to guess at, The Irish Immigrant Pub. In addition to Geelong, Richmond guernseys were purchased by the club at a discount rate from Burley Sekem. Junior development was providing challenge in 1999 but the Cats had no media coverage at that time. Yet, it found a permanent ground in late August of that year, giving it opportunities to effectively base the team. The Cats are keen to promote the pies from a local shop, which is in Matthew Muller's opinion, "the best pies he has ever tasted in the USA or Australia, for that matter."

It is true to say in the continuing story of this improving club that the best is yet to come from the Seattle Cats. The current leaders are: President, Matthew Muller; Coach, Andrew Donlen; Vice Presidents, Jim Trenerry.

The ever resourceful leaders of Seattle decided on yet another name change for the year 2003. They are now known as the Seattle Grizzlies.

THE CENTRAL REGION CLUBS

The current Central Region Clubs are: Chicago Swans, Chicago Sharks, Cincinnati Dockers, Dallas Magpies, Kansas City Power, Louisville Cats, Milwaukee Bombers, Minnesota Freeze, Nashville Kangaroos, St.Louis Blues, San Antonio and Western Mariners.

The inaugural USAFL national champion club, the Cincinnati Dockers, is discussed in Chapter 4.

Chicago Swans

The Chicago Mob was created June 1998 playing under that name for its inaugural season. The name went along with the gangster tag that Chicago has been carrying since the days of Capone. In 1999 the team name was changed to The Chicago Swans, reflecting its affiliation with the Sydney Swans of the AFL. In 1999 it played in twenty-one games, including three tournaments, recording a tally of 14 wins and 7 losses. It is proud that this record ranked the Swans eighth of the 28 teams that existed nationally at that time. It played local teams like Cincinnati, Kansas City, Milwaukee and St. Louis and journeyed afar to play New York, Denver and Santa Cruz. Denver and Los Angeles were added to its list of opponents in the year 2000. In 1999 the Sydney Swans sent the players jumpers, shorts and socks worn by the Sydney players during the Ansett Cup Preseason Competition. It was very proud when Scott Callahan agreed to help, especially in sponsoring the International Match with Canada on August 1st. Callahan was the Jacobs Creek wine representative. The team was fortunate to secure facilities at the Naperville Central High School completely free of charge. On July of that year the Swans made a successful trip to the Kansas City Tournament where it played well but was beaten in the final by a very good Denver side. By this time, too, it had 28 players on its lists, half American, half Australian. AFL legend, Paul Roos, conducted a training weekend and chief junior developer, Jeff Norris, continued to support the game through clinics and an outstanding summer camp in July. There is little doubt it is one of the pioneering teams in the establishment of USfooty in the United States. In the 2000 season it planned a full season of teams leading up to the Nationals in October in Los Angeles. During that season, it had 19 wins and 5 losses. Unfortunately, two of those five were to San Diego and Santa Cruz in the Nationals in Los Angeles, but the Swans had had two good wins overcoming New York by four goals and Cincinnati by three goals.

Sponsorship had been successful with AT&T Wireless, Goose Island Brewery, SouthCorp Wines (Penfolds) and funds from a charity walk which boosted its finances.

Social activities included an Indoor Cricket challenge against the Milwaukee Bombers and an awards banquet with a Halloween theme.

Junior development, through Jeff Norris's promotions and schools visits, occurred. The players were proud that Ron Miller and Shawn Danhauser were selected for the Revolution team to play Canada. It is significant that Ron Miller had played 50 games for the Swans by the end of the 2000 season. Josh Dunn equaled that performance by October 14th in the National Champions. The ambitious Swans planned a 25-game schedule in 2001.

Although we did not include this important club in Chapter 4 with our five champion teams, National President, Rich Mann, suggested that it belonged with the elite teams. And from the strength of the Chicago organization, it is likely it will soon move up into that category. There is little doubt; the Swans are one of the pioneering teams in the establishment of Australian Rules Football in the United States.

In the year 2002 the board consisted of: Andrew Latessa (President), Alistair Maculation (Vice President), Ken Dorn (Secretary), Todd Holmberg (Treasurer), Jeff Fisher and Rob Wilson (Marketing Coordinators), Paul McMahon (Assistant for Junior Development), Rich Noty (Webmaster), Carl Brazen dale (Head Coach), Paul McMahon and Alistair MacGlasham (Assistant Coaches), Julian Callachor, Dan Walsh, Dan Kastihan and Pete Ternes (General Committee). In 2003, the club listed the following contacts: Andrew Latessa (President), Alistair Maculation (Vice President), Todd Holmberg (Treasurer), Carl Brazen dale (Head Coach), and Jeff Norris (Junior Development).

Chicago Sharks

Bursting upon the scene as if summoned from the depths, calling themselves "Sharks" and all potential opponents "Shark Bait," they played their first 2003 tournament in February. It seems they intend to be versatile in fielding both nine-per-side and eighteen-per-side teams where appropriate. This dedicated bunch trained for five weeks in sub-zero freezing temperatures only to be greeted by a balmy, warmish day in Phoenix. Further to their testing debut was an 8 a.m. start against Orange County Crush which was still not appreciated. They demolished Baltimore/Washington Eagles in that tournament but lost again to a crew known as the Chandler Outlaws. In 2001 the founding fathers of this merry new band were Brett Boyd, Jeff Dreher, Warrick Burgmann, Darren Fernandes, Dan Macias, Craig Miller, Jeremy Morgan, and Jeff Tassi. The Illinois Ironmen faded in 2001 causing these pioneers to move into the center of Chicago and start up the Sharks. They play home games at Waveland Field with official headquarters being located at Durkin's Tavern being located at 810 West Diversey. Spurning the notoriety of AFL provision, they are affiliated with the Southport Sharks of the Queensland Australian Football League. They have recorded numerous losses but wins over Denver B, Chicago Swans, Cincinnati Dockers, the Milwaukee Bombers and the now defunct Illinois Ironmen in 2002 gave them occasion to "life a glass." There is an energy in this club which will bring much joy to the entire USAFL.

Dallas Magpies

In the beginning, this team was founded by Brett Ryan through an internet call for a "kick of the Sherrin" in 1997. In the weeks that followed, many people made this contact, and in May of 1998, the group held the first of our now weekly training sessions. The club's first President, Andrew Holland, worked hard to build the team and increase our numbers. The club formed an Organizational Committee in July of 1999. It embarked on its first playing season in 1999. It was known then as the Dallas Outlaws. Five interclub games were planned with a major trip to Kansas City for a tournament on June 19th of that year. Naturally, all of the problems of a start-up club were experienced: a solid player base and sufficient numbers were amongst its initial concerns. Nine players attended its first training session. It set out to secure a sister club in Australia. Eventually, it succeeded and a name change to the Dallas Magpies was made. It also had problems finding a permanent home and, of course, developing sponsors. During this important season Dallas reached out in friendship to San Antonio where a club was beginning to form. Lots of scrimmages involving its own players and volunteers from San Antonio and Houston were played. Eventually, it played Kansas City Power and squeaked a 7-point victory which gave the Magpies great momentum. Two hundred and fifty people attended the party that night with 6 rugby balls handed out as door prizes. It was a great finale for 1999. As a result of this first season, the Magpies planned modest but important goals. One was to have club matches every month, two to form an organizational committee with club offices, three to play in two major tournaments that year especially against Kansas City Power, Denver Bulldogs, Chicago Swans, Cincinnati Dockers and the St. Louis Blues. Four, it reckoned on being represented in the National Tournament in Los Angles. Five, it realized it had to have American players. Six, the Magpies wanted to increase the game's popularity statewide.

In the first quarter of the year 2000, Collingwood endowed Dallas with the proud name of Magpies. Rich Mann conducted a training session and consummate enthusiasm developed. It was successful in establishing training sessions at the J. J. Pierce High School and began the long task of teaching locals the skills of the game. David Goad developed a quarterly report in such a way that important questions were posed during the developmental phases. Kansas City Power reversed the first-season defeat 77 points to 72. The Dallas Magpies combined with the Illinois Ironmen in that tournament. Like most teams, it experienced player loss in its second year and had to recruit widely to make essential numbers. Also, it needed to get support and, like so many others, directed attention to filling Christy's Sportsbar and Grill for the Grand Final party. Collingwood helped with video tapes and other essential support with typical generosity. The arid conditions of September in Texas, with ugly cracks on their playing grounds, endangered players. These conditions threatened joints and limbs as the fledgling players struggled with the peculiar skills needed for USfooty. The Dallas Magpies web site in late 2000 established 45 new player contacts and 75 new supporters throughout Texas, Arkansas and Louisiana. Today they list 36 players with some precious skins under their belt the period since 1998. They have defeated the Austin Crows, Kansas City Power and a team from New Zealand.

It opened a pledge drive and praised O'Dowds Little Dublin establishment for hosting the Grand Final party.

Detroit Overdrive

The Detroit Overdrive was founded in June of 1999. Practices began the weekend of June 20th. The <u>Detroit Free Press</u> came to the rescue with an article which produced interested players. The team planned to travel to Cincinnati for the tournament on the weekend of 27th to 29th. Initially, it attracted the interest of a sports promoter from New York but this would take time. Junior development programs were also a problem. The club was ambitious. It began negotiations with the City of Detroit for playing its home games in the Tiger Baseball Stadium. The baseballers were ready to quit that stadium so things looked hopeful. It also looked at the Wisener Stadium in Pontiac in Northern Detroit. The <u>Detroit Free Press</u> was helpful and offered a front-page story should the team take off. The enterprising pioneers also sought players from Michigan State University and Eastern Michigan University. The year 2000 was its inaugural season. It started with 19 active members and developed 25 players before the season ended. Training was held twice a week with the sessions beginning at 1 pm and finishing at 3 pm. At this stage, there was interest in a sister club relationship with Hawthorn but that petered out. The initial enthusiasm for the Tiger Stadium collapsed also due to the requirement that it could scarcely secure attendance would give $10,000 a game. This reduced the field to much smaller and more modest venues. In 2000 the club envisaged games with Chicago, Milwaukee, the Ironmen, Denver, Lehigh, Kansas City and the Dockers. However, this club folded early in 2000 and its remaining players joined the Chicago Swans. A new club called the Windsor Mariners (which had never been affiliated with the Detroit Overdrive) was now been formed. This club is based in Windsor, Canada, and is actively recruiting in the Detroit area. The history of this new club can be read in this section of the Central Region Clubs.

Illinois Ironmen

The Illinois Ironmen team is another modest ensemble beginning its existence with precarious stability. As of July 2000 it consisted of 16 players, all American, and little experience. Its record to that time was one win, six losses and one draw. Regularly, it teamed up with other clubs so its players could get experience: Dallas, Milwaukee and the Chicago Swans are those teams. David Martinez was the initial founder and Roy Ramer has kept the spirit of the Ironmen alive by being an active recruiter for the Chicago Swans. The Ironmen is now an extinct team

Kansas City Power

The redoubtable Mark Scott took over the presidency of the Kansas City Power Football Club when Jason Eustice moved to Florida. In six weeks of travel in Australia, he managed to communicate with the affiliated AFL Club, Port Adelaide. He went to the preseason Grand Final in Melbourne and met Gavin Wanganeen and his team. Manager of Football Operations, Rob Snowdon, endowed him with 15 Port Adelaide guernseys and other team paraphernalia. Its first training session was March 20th with Andy Pickard, the Vice President, handling the session. Ten to twelve people turned up to each subsequent session with the club's first game against Chicago and St. Louis occurring on April 17th. The year 1999 was successful although it still was only getting 7-10 players traveling for their initial games. The tournament was a great success. Fosters and a local bar, Freddy Tees, sponsored this important tournament. T-shirts, food and drink and other paraphernalia were dispensed to the locals and the visiting teams were Denver, Chicago, St. Louis, Cincinnati, Dallas and Minnesota. The Power team made it to the semifinals losing to the eventual champions, Denver. The team has only one Australian and that is the aforementioned, redoubtable Mark Scott. Vice President, Andy Pickard, described this tournament as important in the history of the Power Club. Each team consisted of 14 players and a number of combinations were developed. Unfortunately, lopsided scores were experienced in the year 2000 as Denver prepared its run for the National Championship. Denver defeated Chicago in the final.

Power experimented with interesting developmental projects, especially one called the Battle of the Plains. This is a tournament which features semipro gridiron teams such as Colorado Springs and South West Oklahoma. The previous day Power conducted classes in Australian Football to the sixth, seventh and eighth boys. After lunch it did the same to sixth, seventh and eighth girls. To everyone's surprise, the girls went in as hard as the boys. This tournament took place about the same time as September 11th so each participant wore red, white and blue tape on their left arms and black tape on their right arms. It played a couple of shortened exhibition games and entertained the crowd with much gusto. As of January 2002, President, Brian Furr, who was also the best and fairest during the 2001 season, departed Kansas City. Mark Wheeler took over as President of the club. Grant Jennings became Junior Development Coordinator and Power players, Brian Furr and Travis Statlander, were chosen in the American Revolution Team to play in the Atlantic Alliance Cup in London.

Kansas City can safely consider itself to be one of the original pioneers of the game of USfooty. The stability of its organization was attested when it was chosen to run the National Championships in October

2002 and repeat in 2003. Those leading the charge in 2003 are President Dan Vacanti, Vice President Mark Scott and USAFL Delegate Brian Furr.

Louisville Cats

The Louisville Cats came into existence in the summer of 1996 when Louisville resident and Aussie Rules enthusiast, John Harrell, found a spark of interest on the Internet from the Cincinnati area in terms of playing a game of Australian Football. Little did "Papa John" know what was ahead of that first communication. Papa John posted flyers around the Louisville area, and built enough interest to have a 15-man squad ready to play the Cincinnati team in the first-ever game of Australian football played in the United States. Played in Louisville at Cherokee Park Cincinnati defeated the Louisville team 19-19-133 to 1-5-11. Trevor Church and Chris Parsley were also club co-founders. The entire USAFL was shocked to learn of John Harrell's death, aged 36, after a massive stroke. He was one of the illustrious founders not only of the Louisville Football Club but of the USAFL. Tributes poured in from all over the country side, especially from Plugger O'Keeffe, founding President of USAFL, and Mike Powers, President of the Atlanta Kookaburras. It is a tribute to his energies that there are so many clubs forming teams in all areas of the United States today. Current leaders of this club are listed as President Trevor Church, Vice President John Miller and USAFL Delegate John Harrell. John Harrell's contributions continued to the end.

Louisville was the first club in the country to receive assistance from an Australian Football League club, receiving guernseys and footballs from the Geelong Football Club in the fall of 1996. The Cats' finest moment may have come in 1997, when it teamed with the Nashville Kangaroos, then in its formative moments, to finish runners-up in the inaugural National Championships in Cincinnati. However, it languished in 1998. For the first several months of 1999, it had shrunk to just ten active members and needed a significant boost to continue as a viable entity. John Harrell reported on the steps taken by the club to revitalize in 1999. By this time, the directory had risen to 18 players and the club schedule for that year had modestly expanded. He listed eight steps.

1   The recruitment of four former players who had for one reason or another disappeared in 1998.

2   The recruitment of several new players with an accent on athleticism and enthusiasm.
3   Negotiation with the Metro Parks Commission to secure a home field.
4   An upturn in negotiations with local business entrepreneurs for sponsorship.
5   Securing non-profit organization status which would allow the club aggressive fund-raising potential.
6   A re-energized relationship with sponsor club in the AFL, Geelong. They have received training videos and manuals and looked for greater depth of cooperation.
7   A media presence needed to be developed.
8   An interesting objective involved the creation of an indoor soccer team to give the players another avenue to gain match fitness.

Tragically, John Harrell died prematurely in 2003. Many compliments were paid and are listed in the USAFL website.

Louisville's main task was regeneration and it seems the new committee was bent on this direction.

Milwaukee Bombers

The Milwaukee Bombers Football Club was founded in 1998 by Paul O'Keeffe, Dale Parsons and Anne Bolton. Like so many other clubs, it was kick-to-kick at a local Milwaukee high school with some home-sick Aussies. In 1998, it played its first game against Chicago. Today, the roster boasts forty players from Milwaukee, Madison and surrounding areas with the hope that the state of Wisconsin would also rise to the occasion.

In the year 1999 the winter was severe causing no football report to emanate in the early stages from "Brew City." Its players at this stage were 60% Australian to 40% Americans, but in its expanded club it had players from New Zealand, England and Ireland. David Mead reported that later in that year the split of Americans and Australians now more resembled 50/50. Financial problems were experienced and it had difficulty attracting sponsors. Miller Brewing turned them down. Umpires were a major problem when Steve Elliott moved to Santa Cruz, so coach, Rob Parry, stepped up into the umpiring shoes. Also, it had no players in the National team so there was much work ahead. Later that year Milwaukee combined with St. Louis to play the Chicago Swans and found a very difficult shortened season of six months restricted its momentum. By this time it had combined with Madison, Wisconsin, and had expanded the player bench with bigger crowds while still maintaining a 50/50 ratio of Australians to Americans. Like other clubs, it planned a strong AFL Grand Final party at Major Goolsby's in Milwaukee and planned to combine with the Dallas Magpies for an onslaught on the National Championships that year. But it succeeded in having the club registered as B grade in quality and quantity which it modestly categorized the chances with the competition.

In the year 2000 the Bombers entered its third season. It was successful in gaining a national profile and social functions, often centered on the USfooty nationals and the AFL Grand Final. Not unlike other USfooty teams, it had indulged in indoor cricket which was always played at the St James Lutheran School. Two local bars, the Oak Crest Tavern in Madison and Mini's Tavern in Milwaukee, came to the rescue financially. The Bombers lost David Mead, a founder and a past president of the club, in 2000. He suffered from the recognizable disease of "returning to Australia." But two games were reported on in a local Madison newspaper. It was pleased when sister club, Essendon, won the AFL Premiership but rued the possibility of having to change club colors because the old match jumpers were passing into dotage. The year 2000 saw on-field performances as middling with yet another possibility of having to combine with another club for the National Championships. It was pleased to report that Gary D'Amato of the Journal Centinel staff took an important interest and penned an article called, "Kicking Some Behinds, Australian Rules Football Gaining a Foothold in Milwaukee." A story on "Plugger" also appeared in Milwaukee's Business Journal.

In addition to a virile social calendar, the Bombers also have a newsletter which is called "The Talking Stick." In keeping with its dual pre-occupation, Milwaukee and Wisconsin, its board represents both states. Plugger O'Keeffe is on this board along with Gary Hill past coach of the national team, The Revolution. The other board members are: Rob

Parry (Milwaukee); Chris Adams (Madison); Jason Becker (Madison); Stuart Smith (Madison)

Milwaukee had an excellent 2002 winning the local AFL Grand Final and playing in the Division 3 Nationals Grand Final. Plugger was back in the President's chair which was welcomed by all. It is appropriate to include a story by Jim Cryns in the short take with the title, "Footy and Froth."

"It's nothing like the American type of football we're used to watching. And, 'it's nothing like rugby,' says Paul O'Keeffe, footy player and public relations director for the Milwaukee Bombers. 'Footy is comprised of a combination of elements that doesn't resemble any other sport.'

"The Milwaukee Bombers is a footy team that plays Australian Rules Football on Milwaukee area fields. "Footy" is much faster and higher scoring than football. The contest is fluid, with no line of scrimmage. 'There's a ball advancement called "handballing," as you might see in volleyball,' O'Keeffe explains. 'There is a "ruck contest" which resembles a tip-off in basketball.' Footy focuses on the pursuit of the ball; there's no padding allowed and players don't hit as hard as they would in a football game. Most games are played at Kletszch Park on the N. Milwaukee River Parkway.

"Here's how the game works. A match is divided into four 20-minute periods. A goal is scored when the ball is kicked through two goal posts, just like a field goal. Goals are six points each. The team in possession of the ball works to advance it by either "handballing" it (volleyball style) or kicking it downfield. They may s also run with the ball as long as they bounce it every ten meters. The team scores six points for kicking the ball through the middle of four posts and one point for kicks inside the outer two posts.

"Australian Football has a club-based structure. The Bombers will sometimes gather at Mini's on Green Bay Road after a game. 'It's a grassroots game that allows players to interact with the Australian culture.' O'Keefe relates. 'Guys go to a pub after the game and have a beer together. Right now, the footy teams in this country are comprised of 70 percent American players and the remainder Australians. Since 1997, the league in the United States has grown from eight to 35 clubs today.

"It's not essential for an individual to have ever played a sport before, much less starred in a sport in college or school. 'We don't have players try out for footy.' O'Keeffe explains. 'All we ask are they turn up at practice. If you turn up for practice you will play in the game.'

"'We don't talk a lot about fitness.' O'Keeffe says. 'Training is relatively easy, but you should be prepared to run about for a fair amount of time.' These guys as players run an average of twelve miles over the course of the game. Practices are held at MSOE Sports Field as well as Kletszch Park. If you would like to learn more about footy in Milwaukee, if you would like to attend a game, or even sign up to play, visit www.milwaukeebombers.com and take it from there."

Minnesota Freeze

The Minnesota Freeze reported in 2000 that the team was alive and well. Spokesman, Anthony Davis, admitted the club was not yet well organized but was optimistic and appealed for new players. Actually, the Freeze began in 1999. Four months of training and skills sessions appealed to 12 people who were excited to get into the game. A couple of these team members went to Kansas City Tournament and played for the Dallas Outlaws. It was hoping to get more involved in Milwaukee and Chicago before planning to send some players to the Nationals Championships in Cincinnati. It was proud of the efforts of one umpire, Steve Arnott, who is considered one of the best umpires in the country. The team was also excited about a physical education and social studies course that incorporated Australian Football in their schools. This caused Freeze to contact the legendary Jeff Norris who helped it with strategies for development. Further, it reported contact with the St. Croix Secondary School developed in the Stillwater area schools. One enterprising promoter felt that learning through participation in Australian Rules Football is not only a social activity but has scholastic possibilities as well. It is not without interest that we note the Minnesota Freeze can come up with intriguing ideas when the great thaw sets in. Although we get reports from time to time that the Minnesota Freeze is frozen in time, break-outs seem to occur so burial rights will not occur at this time.

Nashville Kangaroos

The Nashville Kangaroos are proud, very well organized and possessive of a collective sense of humor. Throughout its history it has fought with Plugger over a range of issues involving the constitution, the national championships, the rules and the respective competitions. Much of the brawling, however, has been tongue-in-cheek with the establishment of USfooty the first objective. The Kangaroos are proud of their history. Most clubs would say that it experienced watching a football game and "a club broke out." With Nashville the shenanigans of the local pub were well established before it was decided that a "football team should break out." The organization actually began in 1994 as a social group watching Australian Rules Football on television and continued this way until 10997 when a few local Aussies and a Chicago native took to a local park and started kicking a footy around.

It was in December 1997 that the Nashville Kangaroos became an official club. That year it traveled to Washington and then Cincinnati to play in the first-ever national tournament in the USA. Its best performance was a top five finish in the 2000 national championships in Los Angeles. A not-for-profit organization, incorporated in 1998, lists three missions:

1. To promote Australian Football;
2 To promote the largest Australian festival in North America;
3. To promote Australian–American relations.

The Roos were keen to include all interested Americans and are supported by a booster club which is active and influential. It is true to say that the Nashville people have a grand vision and a long-sighted view for USfooty. Every September there is an Australian festival held in Nashville. It is planned to occur at the same time the AFL's Grand Final is conducted. There is a televised performance for all to see in addition to a festival which includes a Grand Final party, an Australian Football tournament and a black tie Australian Football ball to add to the celebratory atmosphere. The festival has been featured on national television and as a feature on local television, named simply as "G'day".

The club's president, Shane Clohesy, was supported by an enthusiastic board and a longtime coach John Nelson who was replaced by

Grant White in 2002. Ruth Freeland was the Secretary and John Brinker was the Football Manager.

Nashville has had some great wins in their tenure. With the help of six players from Cincinnati it downed Boston in the first game of 1999 in Nashville. It was a thriller that went down to the last moment with just one goal separating the teams.

Former USAFL President, Rich Mann, favored placing the Nashville team in Chapter 4. The authors agreed that Nashville is a signature club and would soon be joining the national champions on that elevated pedestal. Certainly, it has been active in establishing the Mid American Australian Football League (MAAFL). This divisional organization like the CAFL is an important development giving local teams an opportunity to win in their local spheres. It is also important in that financial constraints do not prevent teams from playing full schedules. Nashville is the kind of team that develops history and tenure and the authors are sure it will not be long before it belongs in the elite teams of USfooty. Through the continuing efforts of Peter Beare whose BeareWare computer industry is strong in support of the Kangaroos, they have developed a formidable program of Australiana in the Nashville area.

Office Directors for 2003 were Shane Clohesy (Chairman/President), Jeffrey Persson (Treasurer), Amy Link (Secretary), Grant White (Coach), Dee Vsetecka (Captain), John Brinker (Football Manager), .

St. Louis Blues

When Sam Ingram, a life-long Carlton supporter, met up with Dave Nicholls in early 1997, they discovered, naturally, over a few beers, that they were both from Melbourne, born one week apart and barracked for Carlton and Collingwood, respectively. They both realized that a deep hole existed in the American environs, the presence of Australian Football. Hence, the St Louis Blues were born, becoming the seventh team to join the United States Australian Football Association which is now the United States Australian Football League.

Initially it experienced problems that many other clubs encountered; e.g., the size of the ground. It then had to find players. The Blues first training run was held at McNair Park with two Aussies and two Americans attending. "Every man and his dog" became its recruiting philosophy. By June 1997, it played its first official game against Kansas City winning a thriller by four points. Naturally, Sam Ingram worked to establish a sister club relationship with that great AFL club Carlton (The Blues). St. Louis received a set of "navy blue" uniforms from its sister club.

Four years down the track, recruiting is still one of the most difficult aspects of a successful footy team. However, the club does boast a more mature bunch of experienced American players who now form the nucleus of this proud club. And, like in the beginning, what brings the team together is the enjoyment of the game of football and the camaraderie that can be shared over a cool beverage. Although experiencing small numbers at training, it went through undefeated in its first year. Club officers in 2002 were James Martin, President; Matt Arrandale; Christian Mullgardt, Secretary; Cameron Murray, Treasurer.

San Antonio Diablos/San Antonio Football Club/Austin Crows

The San Antonio Diablos began with a spirit that has to be admired. In a report by Miles Sims, we read,

"We've only been at it a few weeks so we are still heavily in a recruiting mode. We had six at this week's practice and we are expecting twelve next week. We haven't yet unleashed a PR marketing campaign yet we are encouraged. Our biggest drawback is that we have no one who has even played a minute of footy so we all run around kicking and bouncing a ball like madmen. I think we may be one of the few clubs with no Aussies involved. That said, footy is still the greatest sport on the planet."

With this attitude the San Antonio Football Club was formed. A web site was struck and a two-tier platform introduced. The first tier concerned club level participation with a focus on social enjoyment. The second tier involved the fielding of a team which could eventually compete in regional and national tournaments. To its credit, it attracted two sponsors, Clockwork Design Studio and Radar.com. Pepsi threw in some sponsorship also. It located playing fields, and then wrestled with the concept of ground size, portable goals and a method of designating the boundaries. Most matches in the first year were intramural, although it did plan two games against Dallas. The web site is also appealing.

Ultimately, this group of Southern Texans included players from as far afoot as Ireland to Kenya so they became the Austin Crows. Miles Simms is President and Steve Gaines is Vice President. They associate strongly with Austin's sister city in Australia, Adelaide, and have some players from that fair town.

Windsor Mariners

windsor mariners australian football club

The Windsor mariners were formed by Adrian Parry in late 2001 after discovering the Canadian Australian Football Association (CAFL) and the Ontario Australian Football League (OAFL) on the web. After a story appeared in the <u>Windsor Star</u> concerning the formation of the team, the club was formed with a squad of 18 players. After some initial disappointments, the club announced that Malden Park was to be the home of the Mariners. The 2002 season, the first for the club in the OAFL, was somewhat of a disappointment. The club had player number problems that forced it to forfeit all away games, leaving only 7 games for the season. The club finished with a 1-13 record, and was last on the OAFL ladder. The club has made some changes during the off-season, and is now emerging stronger than ever and looking forward to the coming 2003 season.

Adrian Parry (Windsor Mariners AFC President and founding member) continues the story: "While the club is based in Windsor, Ontario, we are the official team for Detroit and the state of Michigan. We can, if we so choose, play in the US Nationals each year, and have started recruiting in Detroit, with 5 players added to our roster (all Australians). At this time, we are more concerned with building a strong club, so that we do not share the fate of the Overdrive, than in playing in the US National series. However, we are attempting to form some kind of Great Lakes Invitational Cup to be held here in Windsor, and are intending on inviting teams from Chicago, Milwaukee and other nearby communities. Further down the road the club plans to begin a new Detroit side, to play in the OAFL if at all possible, and have interest in forming a junior league between Windsor and Detroit. Our goal is to create 4 junior teams in the Motor City, with a further 2 junior teams here across the border. Once that is accomplished, we can look into building a new Detroit team."

The Mariners are a Canadian team with one foot in the celebrated American city of Detroit.

Wichita

Tom Oxley had this to report. He started trying to get a club together in the summertime, succeeding in attracting 20 people by September 20^{th,} 2000. It was a university ensemble with practices starting on September 28th. Great enthusiasm was displayed. Two Australians contacted him but due to scholarship requirements could only play in November. They did help with practices. The Wichita Club seems to be in a lengthy holding pattern.

THE EASTERN REGION

The Eastern Region has proven to be a strong gathering of independent and proud clubs that stretch from Florida to Buffalo. Strong rivalries have developed in a short time. The Boston Demons are discussed in Chapter 4. The clubs listed are as follows:

Atlanta Kookaburras

The Atlanta Kookaburras Club has existed since 1998 and has thrived in the famous state called Georgia. Atlanta received its nickname from a Nashville supporter based on their loud and oafish behavior; calling them "a bunch of drunk and laughing jackasses." The laughing jackass of the animal kingdom in Australia – the Kookaburra – was hence adopted. Mike Powers reported in 1999, however, that the progress was slow with just four to eight people turning up to practice. It showed initiative in placing advertisements in such communications as Creative Loafing, Atlanta Sports Magazine and the newsletter for the local Aussie Women's Club. Qualcomm, Inc. was the first sponsor and the Club used the local high school's soccer fields (Druids Hills High School) for its games and practices. In 1999, the Kookaburras participated in the South Carolina tournament, a North Carolina tournament, and the Nashville

Grand Final Festival. Atlanta then combined with the Tri-City Saints and the South Carolina Hawks to form the Southern Crusaders for the 1999 National Tournament, wisely electing to play in Division II. The combined team took second place, narrowly defeated by Washington/Lehigh Valley. Georgia's humidity was problematic in July and August with some players traveling 60 miles to attend the Atlanta practices. Attempts were made to hold practices in Athens and succeeded in so far as seven players turned out on September 12, 1999.

In the year 2000 things started with a bang. It called itself the Southeastern Australian Rules Champions with victories over immediate rivals such as Dallas, Milwaukee, Tri-Cities, New York and North Carolina. The performances, however, in the Los Angeles National Championships were ordinary. It was narrowly defeated in Washington by the fast finishing New York Magpies who topped the B-grade competition on that occasion. The Kookaburras played their home games at Piedmont Park, which is affectionately known as "The Quarry" because of the large volume of rocks and loose gravel. The prominent location got them a lot of curious onlookers. They moved to a field in Conyers which was a better field on which to play but attracted fewer onlookers. Atlanta played well from March through September in 2001 registering a 7-1 win/loss record. Their performance in the Los Angeles National Championships was solid. They qualified for the finals and were eliminated by the eventual champion – the Denver Bulldogs.

In 2001, the Kookaburras almost had to begin anew because they had lost nine players/members to relocation including their coach – Jason Lehman. Again they struggled for numbers and their record was indicative of their lack of depth. Entering the Washington, DC National Championship, Atlanta's record was a 4-5 win/loss and, therefore, they were relegated to the Division II bracket. At the Nationals the Kookaburras came to life progressing to the Grand Final where the team they was narrowly overtaken by a fast finishing New York Magpies for the Division II Championship.

The year 2002 saw the Kookaburras build upon the prior years' momentum. Atlanta has secured significant sponsorship from Visy Recycling and Coca-Cola. It has also managed to raise funds with memberships and the selling of memorabilia and paraphernalia, especially a delightful rain-soaked picture in the <u>Atlanta Journal Constitution</u>. They have managed media support with local radio and newspapers. The

Kookaburras are confident that Australian Football has arrived permanently in the sweet State of Georgia. The Kookaburras repeated as champions of the SEAFL in 2002. Just like in Australia where communities get behind their teams, practice and game days are also very much social outings. That would explain the team motto, "Play some footy, drink some beer, and have some laughs."

At the end of 2002, the following club officers were Mike Powers (President), Heath Moore; (Vice President), Justin Biggs; (Treasurer), Marty Hyder; (Coach, Lou Fullager); Assistant Coach, (Wayne Kraska); and Recruiting Manager, (B. J. Gambaro).

Baltimore/Washington Eagles

The Washington Eagles team has been around since 1997 when it became runners up in the first Australian Football Champions of the United States. In 1998 it hosted the Boston Demons for the first game of the year in Washington. The team disintegrated during that year but they bounced back in '99 to a respectable ensemble. Dave Schall, co-webmaster of the new combined team takes up the description.

"12-01-02 - It all started one spring day back in 1999 with a friendly challenge between the Australian Embassy in Washington, D.C. and a popular bar called the Boomerang Pub run by a bunch of entrepreneurial Australians up in Baltimore. With the help of a few guys from Lehigh Valley, the day took off in splendid fashion on a shredded, American football field in Baltimore. Hits were hard and the sweat flowed passionately as many ex-pats shook off the cobwebs and Americans adjusted to the rules of this new sport. In the end, the home squad, the Baltimore Bombers, beat out the Washington Eagles quite convincingly; 11.6:72 to 8.7:55. An after-the-game social function held at the Boomerang Pub topped the night off with everyone having a great time. However, more important than what was on the scoreboard were the seeds that were sown on the field that day, which eventually grew into the Baltimore Washington Eagles Australian Rules Football Club.

"The Washington Eagles came about in 1997 from a phone call by Jason Eustice out in Kansas City who put up a challenge for D.C. to pull together a football team based out of the Embassy to play his

Midwest All-stars Team. This challenge was taken seriously by the Embassy of Australia and at a regular end of week meeting several members discussed the possibility of putting a team together over a few cold Australian refreshments. They went on to recruit a group of 19 players as well as contacted the West Coast Eagles back in Australia about helping out with jumpers and other equipment. With new jumpers in hand and a good group of guys, the Eagles were ready to start shaking and moving.

"The Baltimore squad came together through Steve Hupparty, who owned and managed the Boomerang Pub in downtown Baltimore. With an Australian theme, the Boomerang was one of Baltimore's most unique and popular restaurants. With the challenge coming from the Embassy to field a team full of Aussies and Yanks, the Boomerang put together a winning team in a matter of a couple weeks.

"After that day, the Eagles then joined up with USFooty, a newly formed league of Australian Rules teams spanning the entire United States. We built our own committee and bylaws, we developed a team composed of Baltimore and D.C. players as well as the occasional Lehigh Valley player, and we began our journey with matches against New York and Nashville, as well as traveling out to Cincinnati that August for the National Tournament. Proud to say, the Eagles flew high that weekend, winning top honors in the second division (the newer teams to the league):

"With trophy in hand, and a name made for being a "social team" as well as a "footy team," the Eagles spent the 2000 season working hard at developing our roster and teaching those not familiar with the game, the essentials (kicking, handballing, shepherding, etc.). With matches against Lehigh Valley, North Carolina, Nashville, Boston, Philadelphia, Tri-Cities/Atlanta and even the Lawrence Park Rebels (a Canadian team that trekked down to play), the Eagles grew stronger with every game both mentally and physically.

"In the fall of 2000, the Eagles put a team together to travel out to Los Angeles to play in the USAFL National Championships in Division I. Though we brought a good squad to the grounds and we did put up a fight, beating Phoenix and Orange County, the Eagles fell in key matches against Atlanta and Denver (Denver later won the National Tournament Championship).

"With a bitter taste in our mouths from the 2000 Nationals, the Eagles set about taking the next step and becoming more of a premiere team. We put in a bid to host the 2001 Nationals; we moved out of the Boomerang Pub and built ourselves an official three-room clubhouse, and we looked at hosting even more fundraising events to help sponsor the club financially. The Eagles had never worked as hard before, not only in organizing our club, but also playing games against New York, Lehigh Valley, Boston and Philadelphia twice, North Carolina, playing in the Chicago Tournament against the Chicago Swans, Kansas City and Milwaukee before getting set for the 2001 Nationals, which we hosted in our own backyard at Rosecroft Raceway, outside Washington, D.C. Focusing on entertaining our guests, 20 teams, we also sported a side that was extremely hard-working and persistent."

The organization of the USfooty National Championships by the Eagles was splendid with twenty teams turning up to compete for championship honors. It was a gala festival with the games beginning at 8 am on Saturday October 13 and finishing at 4.30 pm on October 14. Organizers drew a raffle during the Grand Final at half time that sent two people to Australia and further raffles contributed food, wines and aboriginal artifacts to the lucky recipients. A feature of its down-under immersion was the relish of vegemite sandwiches available from the stalls throughout the tournament. Many of the attending football teams experienced the joys of harness racing in the evenings. Retiring USAFL President, Rich Mann, has been especially praising of this club. It is incorporated, has instituted a professional finance system, obtained a sponsorship from Marlborough and the Boomerang Club in Baltimore, a local cable company, The Kangaback Enterprises, along with private sponsors like Paul Shea and Richard Chung. They seem capable of attracting modest amounts from a wide number of supporters: Hardy's Wines, Zepher Inc. Security Company, the Australian Embassy Social Club and even such groups as the Australian Street Festival.

The Eagles did not fare well at the 2002 Nationals at Kansas City where they finished bottom of Pool B in Division 2. Webmaster, David Schall, however, was upbeat about the future of the ensemble.

"For the 2002 season, the Eagles were spent. We lost the clubhouse in Baltimore, but gained another pub in Herndon, Virginia called Ned Devine's Ned Kelly's. There, we enlisted the pub's support and did heavy recruiting building on a diminishing Baltimore roster.

"We decided to spend time developing the team itself, establishing METRO games against ourselves in order to develop our skills and improve whereas training alone could not. We also became part of the NEAFL (Northeast Australian Football League) which the USAFL established on location. Two divisions in this new league would make competition against other "more local" teams easier. In our division were Boston and New York, with the other division composed of Lehigh Valley, Philadelphia and Western Pennsylvania. Rules for the NEAFL were that we play everyone at least once, while playing teams in our division twice (a home/away series). We also were proud to have three of our members travel down to Australia to play in the inaugural International Cup. Our coach Denis Ryan was the head coach for the U.S. squad, with players Jay Hunter (U.S.) and Robbie Brunton (Canada) representing their countries in a month-long tournament held in Melbourne. With that said, we jumped at the chance to fly out to Kansas City and partake in the 2002 Nationals. There we were mixed in with the Second Division group and played hard against teams from Santa Cruz, a combined squad from Phoenix and Lehigh, and St. Louis. Unfortunately due to lack of preparation and turnouts at trainings, the Eagles fell to the basement of their division.

"However, momentum is definitely turning better for the 2003 season. We've established a new pub up in Baltimore to help build and recruit that side, we're doing heavy recruiting down in D.C. and Northern Virginia, we've got a new committee who's fresh and ready to work, a new look for our website that's easier, more information and more timely to read up on, and a new schedule that pits the Eagles against NEAFL talents as well as traveling on the road."

Officials for the 2003 season were Rob Brunton (President), Paul McIntyre (Vice President of Washington), Dave Schall (Vice President of Baltimore), Michael Fay (Treasurer), Jay Hunter (Head Coach), and Denis Ryan (Assistant Coach).

Buffalo

Buffalo is one of those teams that are still under development. This has not changed.

Florida

Jason Eustice reported that intrepid characters were in the process of organizing the club in Tampa and Orlando. There were three of them involved in 1999. By the year 2000 they had their first get-together in March 25th in Orlando. Thirteen guys turned up, eleven Australians and two Americans. They organized a game with six a side. The heat was a problem, the game a success. The standard of play was encouraging with some passages of play described here in its report as "nice." One of the problems of this early group was distance as the players came from a number of cities. It had balls provided by the USAFL and other promotional materials but it needed jumpers and sources of sponsorship. Florida is correctly described as under development.

In 2002 there were at least three Florida contacts making up almost 80 members of this team now known as the Florida Redbacks. There were contacts in North Florida, Orlando and Fort Lauderdale/Miami. A huge crowd turned up to see their game with Atlanta where television and newspaper coverage added greatly to interest in the State of Florida. Their invitation philosophy is "Come out and have a kick with us." A contact pub is the Cock and Bull. The Redbacks' committee was as follows: Marc Karver (President), Jason Eustice (Vice President and Captain), Ben Hancock (Marketing and Promotions), Trevor Stokes (Coach), John McAlister (Treasurer), and John Angel (Webmaster).

Green Mountain Eagles/ Vermont Eagles

The Green Mountain Eagles was newly formed in 2001 and have a sister relationship with the Vermont Eagles in Melbourne, Australia. Its regular training is every Wednesday, after which they meet for drinks at the Banana Winds pub near the Fort Ethan Allen ground. Banana Winds offer a "buy one beer get one free" deal for every Australian Rules player. The team has played against teams such as Boston Demons, Brewster Academy, New York Magpies, and Nashville Kangaroos.

Lehigh Valley Crocodiles

The Crocodiles are an unique ensemble in that most of its original players are recruited from the Nazareth area high schools. The players call themselves "the best little team in USfooty" and if youth is a criterion, their claims are accurate and they've been around for some time, being formed in April 1999. Veteran coach, Robert Giabardo had arrived from the New York Magpies, so his interest was already established. After moving to Nazareth, Pennsylvania, where he was Assistant Track and Field Coach of the Nazareth area high school, he decided to form a local club rather than commute two hours to New York City. This story is worth relating. Robert, an ex Victorian, gave an Australia Day Lecture to 320 eighth grade students in Nazareth, Pennsylvania. Much interest was sparked and many students asked many questions. No, the game was not like rugby. So Rob invited them to join him in the spring when the snow had melted. The first practice was scheduled for later March 1999 with one student showing up. His wife then, Michelle, persuaded him to persist. With flyers posted in the Middle School and the High School and a promise of mid-week training sessions, the numbers increased to 10 and more. The school district on April 12th gave permission for the club to become officially called the Lehigh Valley Crocodiles. Growing pains were experienced. Funds were meager. Footballs and videos were needed. Attracting Americans to play this strange game was not easy. The nearest club was New York who, fortunately, proved extremely supportive. On May 8th, the first ever game with New York at the Nazareth High School, materialized. It was a great success. A trip to Baltimore improved the learning curve impressing the Eagles with the enthusiasm and the quality of their play. It played Philadelphia who proved no match for the young fit legs of the Lehigh Valley team. Graduation decimated the squad but before it could become discouraged, suddenly, out of nowhere, so to speak, a set of old jumpers from Rob's old club, The Hampton Rovers, arrived. Accompanying this Godsend was another box with junior development materials from the Prahran Dragons. Prized content was a new Sherrin football. It was now a real football team. An eleven a side tournament involving New York and Washington/Baltimore occurred on Saturday, 18th of September, 1999. One of the games at this tournament against New York Magpies was a classic. The tournament achieved its objective. The young students were now keen to promote their club. The team continued to play New York and Atlanta with mixed success and had the good fortune of supplying the first scholarship winner, Dustin Jones, for the trip to Australia with a three-week training stint under Kevin Sheedy and the Essendon Bombers. Two years later Josh Loring was named the 2002 Player Scholarship winner. Coach Giabardo was named National Under 23 Head Coach with Assistant Coach Les Thomas and 7 players included in the squad. The Lehigh Crocs are justly proud of their accomplishments in the four years of their existence.

The board of directors reflected a union of students, teachers and local businessmen: President, Joshua Loring; Vice President, Adam Nowicki; Secretary, Les Thomas; Treasurer, Jeremy Silimperi; Board member, Jason Amstutz; Member at Large, Mike Miller. In 2003 the Board members were Josh Loring (President), Les Thomas (Secretary), Rob Giabardo (Treasurer), and Elaine Thomas (Member At Large).

New Hampshire

This team started out as a group of teachers from Brewster Academy, who then got people from the local community to join them. The team has played a few games at the Academy in Wolfboro with the Boston Demons which has a good ground for Australian football. As the game is followed by a barbecue, it has also been a family social gathering for the two clubs. This event will continue to be an annual event. The team is made up of 90% Americans. Doug Algate is the person to contact for details.

New York Magpies

This club was established in March of 1998. Not long after it played its first football game against the Boston Demons in Boston at Babson College. This established a tradition of rivalry that is the strongest in the eastern region and one of the classic competitions in USfooty. The year 1999 was vintage in that it defeated Boston for the first time in New York.

Unfortunately, it could not carry this good form into the National Championships and the Magpies were disappointed with the results.

The main focus in the first quarter of year 2000 was to develop an administrative framework that could help the club operate and develop.

Not-for-profit status was high on the club goals. An ambitious schedule was planned which included games with mostly Eastern Division clubs. The players also became more aggressive with media intervention and managed an article in the <u>New York Times</u>. Like so many other clubs, it developed a mutually beneficial relationship with a bar named Dewey's Flat Iron. A permanent home venue still eluded the club but the social activities were picking up and it was working on ways to increase relationships with sister club, the Collingwood Magpies. Positive results were gained by the end of 2000 when it found a new home in Manhattan. The not-for-profit corporation status was now in hand so approaches for sponsorship had muscle. It treasured the Anzac Cup Competition with Boston and Philadelphia where it was always competitive. Without a doubt, its finest moment since its establishment of 1998 was the premiership earned in USAFL Division 2 in Washington in 2001. The Magpies trailed at half-time by almost 2 goals but rallied in the second half to hold the Atlanta Kookaburras scoreless while adding three goals to its own tally. The New York Magpies were now ready for elevation to Division 1 in 2002 and proud of its new found winning spirit. Initially, the Magpies experienced difficulty in recruiting Americans, but that changed during the 2001 season. The committee for 2002 was as follows: The President, Peter Gurry; Vice President, Tom Thompson; Secretary, Matt Barlaz; Treasurer, Tom Thompson; Coach, James Patterson; Recruitment Officer, Simon Bell; Assistant Recruitment Officer, Ed Clancy; Acting Field Czar, Hamish Anderson; Social Chairman, Erik Kalhovd; Public Relations, Nic Denyer; Nor-for-profit Counsel, Curt McDonald; Web Master, Simon Miller. For the 2003 season the following were the office bearers: Peter Gurry (President), Doug Lewis (Vice President), Gary Lerch (Treasurer), Jon McClelland (Secretary), James Paterson (Coach), Erik Kalihovd (Assistant Coach), Tom Thompson (Operations Manager), Andrew Bridges and Rob Kelly (Metro League Coordinators), Sean Keenan (Marketing Manager), James Paterson (Recruitment Manager), James Malackey, Sam Reid, Mark Kelly, Simon Bell, Michael Robertson, and Chris McIntyre (Social Managers).

North Carolina Tigers

The North Carolina Tigers team was founded by Seth McElvaney in November 1997, with the first training session in early spring 1998. McElvaney, an American, figured that the time was right for footy in the Triangle area of North Carolina.

The first annual committee meeting of the North Carolina Tigers was held in September of 1998. Seth McElvaney was elected president, Len Fullager became Vice President and the Treasurer was David Collins. It moved quickly to secure a sister club in the AFL. Initially, its name was North Carolina Crash but in April 1999 Richmond agreed to become the sponsor club. So the Crash became the North Carolina Tigers.

It started with three wins in 1999 against Atlanta, Carolina and Tri-Cities. It was proud of its distribution of nationalities: 50% American, 40% Australian and 5% Canadian and New Zealander. It won the Mount Airy Tournament in June 1999 and sent two players – Don Prost and Rob DiMarco - to Chicago for the U.S. national team's August 1999 match against Canada.

In the fall 1999, members of the Tigers at the University of North Carolina at Chapel Hill founded a club at the university in the hope of growing the game amongst younger members of the community. A second club at North Carolina State University in Raleigh was established a year later, giving Aussie Rules a good foothold among younger Americans in the area.

Its first sponsors were the Aussie Bar and Restaurant in Raleigh and the Down Under Pub in Durham. The Tigers traveled to Nashville in September 1999 for the Grand Final Tournament, losing two games, but many of the club's younger and collegiate members got a good introduction to footy. In the National Championships in October 1999 in Cincinnati, seven Tigers teamed up with the Tri-Cities Saints and the Atlanta Kookaburras to come second as the combined "Southern Raiders" in Division 2.

At the club's second annual general meeting in December 1999, Glenn Fullager was named President; other officers were Martin Coventry (Vice President), Tim Blankemeyer (Secretary), and Seth McElvaney (Treasurer).

North Carolina continued to grow on and off the field in 2000. In October, the club received 27 football jumpers from Richmond Football Club and was proud to finally look like the Tigers and full represent its sister club in Australia. The club is thankful to Terry Grigg of Richmond Football Club for facilitating this donation to the North Carolina Tigers.

The Tigers also strove to be active in the community, participating in Bank of America's "Down Under Tour" of the Triangle area, a celebration of Australia in commemoration of the 2000 Sydney Olympics.

On the field, the Tigers had mixed results early in the season, beating Lehigh Valley, and then losing two out of three matches at the 2000 USAFL Umpires Clinic and Tournament – hosted by the North Carolina Tigers on March 25-26. Despite the results, the clinic/tournament was a great success for the USAFL and for the Tigers, with over 70 players and 11 umpires from across the East Coast and Canada in attendance. The Tigers got a great front-page sports section article on April 4 in the region's primary newspaper, The News and Observer.

The Tigers and the UNC-Chapel Hill university club got great news on June 1, 2000, when Tigers member and UNC-Chapel Hill student, Drew King, was named to the U.S. National Team (The Revolution). King played with the squad against Canada in July 2000. Good things kept happening for the Tigers, as on October 1 in Nashville, North Carolina, recovered from an early tournament loss at the Grand Final Festival, beat the host Kangaroos and won the festival, finishing the 2000 season on a high note.

In November 2000, at the club's third Annual General Meeting, the 2000 board was re-elected for 2001.

The Tigers continued 2001 as strongly as they had finished 2000 on the field, opening the season with five straight wins. In the newly organized Southeastern Australian Football League, North Carolina went undefeated in regular season play, beating the Atlanta Kookaburras and Tri-Cities Saints twice each to finish 4-0. A well-taken home win against Cincinnati finished the excellent five-game run. In the SEAFL Grand Final, however, the Tigers ran into a pumped-up Kookaburras side that took the first ever league title. After splitting two matches at the Boomerang Cup in Baltimore, MD, North Carolina took a strong team to the USAFL National Championships in Division 1, just missing the semifinals. The Tigers finished fifth, a great accomplishment for a young team with so few Australian players. Also, for the first time ever, two players tied for the Tigers' Best and Fairest award. UNC-Chapel Hill student, Scott Cunningham, tied with Martin Coventry for the honors and with Perry Vaughn finishing third.

At the club's fourth Annual General Meeting in December 2001, Tim Blankemeyer was named President, Adam Coleman was named Vice President, Martin Coventry became Secretary and Seth McElvaney remained Treasurer. The club's two-year President and valuable player, Glenn Fullager, returned to Australia with his family in spring 2002, a tough loss for the club. The Tigers are indebted to Glenn for all of his hard work and service since the club's founding; he has since been named North Carolina's liaison to the AFL.

The year 2002 was in many ways was in many ways a transition year for the club. Besides losing Fullager, about ten important members left the club in the off-season, many of whom relocated to other cities in the United States. In addition, the club started a nine-a-side METRO league featuring UNC-Chapel Hill, North Carolina State University and the Raleigh-Durham Eels – a collection of Tigers' older members. This league, the North Carolina Australian Football League (NCAFL), provided the members with more games in the season and increased the visibility of the sport in the region.

The 2002 season kicked off with an NCAFL match on February 23, 2002, between UNC-Chapel Hill and North Carolina State, the first-ever collegiate match in the United States. The more experienced UNC-Chapel Hill team won easily, but the North Carolina State team—with many first timers—acquitted itself well. The match got excellent coverage by the university and local press.

Locally, the Tigers continued to spread the footy gospel, conducting the first-ever youth clinic at a YMCA after-school program at a local elementary school in August 2002. About 30 youngsters got a first-hand introduction to Aussie Rules and the kids and the club had a good time. The Tigers will continue this relationship with the YMCA with future clinics scheduled for 2002 and 2003.

On the field, a now inexperienced Tigers side had an average year results-wise, beating Tri-Cities twice in the regular season SEAFL play, but losing twice to Atlanta and once to Cincinnati. In the SEAFL Grand Final, the Tigers were overwhelmed by Atlanta and the Kookaburras again took the league title.

At the USAFL National Championships in October 18-20 in Kansas City, a 25-member strong Tigers team performed well in Division III, taking two of three matches and losing a tough semifinal match to eventual champion Philadelphia Crows. The trip was a great bonding experience for the Tigers' squad, which looks to get stronger and perform well in 2003. Also, at the event, Tigers' President, Tim Blankemeyer, was named USAFL East Region Vice President.

Philadelphia Crows Become Hawks

Chris Hasson approached the USAFL in late 1988 with the view of having Philadelphia join the new association. His team was accepted and was given the Adelaide Crows as their AFL affiliate. In 1999, the Crows started with great humility – it was in Division C. Nineteen ninety-nine was a year of development and growth for Philadelphia. The first match was played against Lehigh Valley in May with teams of 10 per side. Although the crocodiles won that game, the Crows managed to kick 75 points which is very respectable for a first game. It set up a Tuesday night football night at Dickin's Inn in Philadelphia. Andrew Lochhead became its first coach along with sundry other Australians who helped the club stabilize. Chris Hasson reported that efforts to attract new American players were gaining success and fund raising was concomitant in nature. The idea of playing elevens eventuated from a beautiful rugby field in Marlton, New Jersey. The 2000 schedule included five games and five losses. However, the team rose to Division B and developed team rosters of more than 30 players in that period. Today, it trains twice a week and has excited much interest in the Philadelphia area. It is proud of a strong organization and structure which will soon propel them to greater success.

Committee holders in 2002 were President, Pat White; Executive Director, Lori White; Volunteer-at-Large, Alex Kalajzich; Vice President, Peter Tingate; Ground Operations, Chris Hasson; Assistant, Greg Hodur; Treasurer, Ryan Kavanagh; USAFL Delegate, Andrew Lochhead; Coach, Andrew Lochhead; Social Coordinator, T J Thomas; Interim Sponsorship Coordinator, Peter Tingate; Merchandising, Jack Henderson; Website Administration, Lori White; Assistant, Joe Forsstrom; Publications, Kevin Smith; Assistant, Joe Forsstrom

Although the Crows have had a humble ride through the developmental phase, it has had some wonderful successes. First, there are many Americans and Canadians completing the roster and second, it inflicted the only defeat before the Grand Final on the mighty Boston Demons team in mid season, in Philadelphia in 2001. In 2002, national success attended the Crows when they won Division III championships in Kansas City.

In late 2002 the President of the Hawthorn Club approached the Philadelphia Crows and asked if it was willing to change affiliation to the Hawks. Much discussion was had. The Crows changed affiliation becoming the Philadelphia Hawks. Office bearers for the new club in 2003 were Jack Henderson (President), Peter Tingate (Vice President), Andrew Lochhead (USAFL Delegate).

Raleigh

Raleigh is an offshoot of the North Carolina Tigers with Seth McElveney reporting on its behalf.

South Carolina Hawks

Tony Maher reports that in 1999 the South Carolina Hawks had a schedule and kicked off training by helping Nashville play Boston in March. It played a tournament with Raleigh and Atlanta and in late May 1999 and had a return match in Raleigh. It planned on playing in the September Nashville Grand Final team. On January 23rd the organizational meeting was a trifle disappointing. Only three members turned up. Later, however, it had 15 players on the member list with nine turning up to training regularly and of this listing 45% were American. The local high school called Sanderson High in Raleigh filled in but the club was still searching for a suitable playing field. It had hoped the Richmond Tigers would sponsor it and lend its name, but this did not turn out to be successful. In April 2000 the Hawks talked of finally having a ground on which to play. In July 2000 it played Atlanta and forged an alliance with the local rugby club which allowed better training facilities. Also at that time the Hawks secured a full set of Hawk guernseys with a distinct chance of attracting the Hawthorn Football Club as its sister club. As 2000 came to an end, it lost two games narrowly against Atlanta but was enthusiastic about the third annual meeting which was scheduled for the first week in December.

The Club is currently dormant having lost many Australian members who were the driving forces. Remnants, however, gather frequently for a few rounds in the Pub and occasionally kick the ball around. It mostly contributes players and efforts to help the Tri-City Saints or the Atlanta Kookaburras.

Tri-Cities Saints

The Tri-Cities Football Club keeps appearing in reports of the USAFL from the earliest days. In 1999 it spent most of its time recruiting and preparing for the future. It admits that things have moved slowly. Three reports in the year 2000 by Warren Ballagh indicated that there was "movement at the station." They were exciting times in Tennessee. The previous year it combined with the Carolina Hawks, the North Carolina Tigers and the Atlanta Kookaburras at the Nationals where this combined team were runners up in Division 2. In 2000 they planned to have games in Knoxville against the Louisville Cats and in Atlanta against the Kookaburras. Newspaper articles lifted its profile and enthused patrons. It was very excited with its first sponsor: The Elizabethton Federal Savings Bank donated $50 screened T-shirts so its logo was now prominent. It played the first home game at Milligan College in Johnson City, Tennessee, in the rain. The home team, unfortunately, succumbed to Atlanta and was defeated, but the spirit of the game bode well for the ensuing games, one of which was against the Raleigh Tigers. The Tri-City Saints along with the Kookaburras, the North Carolina Tigers and the South Carolina Hawks formed the Southeast American Football League in 2001. It missed the 2000 Nationals but planned to be active in Baltimore for the 2001 championships. There is a nest of Australian football in the Carolinas that ensures this game will not only continue but thrive in Eastern America. The three cities embodied are Johnson City, Kingsport and Bristol located on the Tennessee border with North Carolina. Several smaller cities and town also contribute to this conglomerate. The President is Warren Ballagh.

Virginia

The Club is currently under formation with Chris Adams from Arlington, Virginia, the information officer. They list no permanent officers as yet but insist that many of the Virginia players are associated currently with the Baltimore/Washington Eagles.

Western PA Wallabies

The Western Pennsylvania Wallabies were founded in 2002 by David Ulonska from Pittsburgh and Scott Strenski from Johnstown. David is an Australian who has been in the U.S. since August 2000, but only moved to Pittsburgh in November 2001. Scott is an American currently residing in Johnstown. Both have a passion for the sport and together formed the Wallabies. Scott and David chose the Wallabies as the team's logo to better associate the club with being an Australian sport. The colors, blue and white, feature prominently in both the Australian and United States' national flags.

The team's leaders in 2002 were President, David Ulonska; Vice President/Club Delegate, Scott Strenski; Secretary, Jeremy Orchard; Social Coordinator, Mel Eperthener; Treasurer, Patrick Higgins; Coach, Jason Bennett.

For 2003 they have scheduled games against other members of the North East Division of the USAFL - Philadelphia Hawks, Lehigh Valley Crocodiles, Boston Demons, Baltimore/Washington Eagles and the New York Magpies. The Executive Committee for 2003 was Scott Strenski (President), David Ulonska (Vice President), Jeremy Orchard (Secretary), Ray Chatfield (Treasurer), Matthew Burke (Marketing, Sponsorships and Merchandising), Scott Magee/David Weisenger (Coach), Simon Lucey/Mike Colligan (Assistant Coach), Jennifer Shrift (Social), and Jocelyn Valley (Website Administrator).

THE STORY OF USfooty

Chapter 6

GEOGRAPHIC DIVISIONS WERE FORMED

America is a very large country and over ninety percent of Americans can and do read stories that interest. Schools claim that all students should be able to read, write, count and understand the properties of a magnet. And from elementary schools through Grade 12 to all kinds of colleges, the American scene is full of this enterprise. Some educators rue the fact that newspapers center their reading levels at Grade 5. This may be so but, at least, most of the newspapers are read, if not cover to cover certainly in the sports sections and on the front pages with the black headlines scanned for both erudition and scandal. It was inevitable that the 50 states would claim uniqueness in some ways and, although 40 clubs forming to play USfooty sounds like a large enterprise, it is really a drop in the bucket when it is realized that there are so many centers of population playing a plethora of sports. The national association, the USAFL, is supported by a growing number of divisional associations. The most visible of these is the Californian Australian Football League or the CAFL. As previously mentioned, most of the Western clubs are members of this league and it has now produced four championship games, the last three of which have been won by San Diego. The Mid American Australian Football League, the MAAFL, began operations in the year 2000. Heavyweights in this division are Nashville, Chicago, Cincinnati and Louisville who played over 40 games between them in the year 2000. Nashville was the winner in the inaugural season. In 2001 Chicago was successful in taking out first prize. The Southeast American Football League began its operations in 2001 with Atlanta winning its very first grand final. Lurking somewhere in the background is yet another organization called: The Australian Football Association of Northern American, AFANA. It has its own board and is mostly interested in lobbying for improved television coverage of the AFL games in the U.S.A. and Canada. Rob DeSantos, who is the CEO of AFANA, maintains its goals are that it is a for-profit corporation which is financed by individual investors, members and from their retail sales. Indeed, it is an official AFL licensee so it pays royalties to the AFL. Its primary mission is to promote Australian Football in the United States and in Canada.

There is a metropolitan league formed by Phoenix. It is an incredibly successful developmental organization, and Los Angeles has formed a similar substrata league in the eager vicinities of that fair city as has the Baltimore/Washington Club.

The last association to form was the Northeast Australian Football League, NEAFL, which held its first championships in 2002. The perennial favorites of this area in the United States, Boston, ended up winning this first title after a titanic struggle with their legendary rivals, New York. The configuration of the main geographical administrative divisions now stands as outlined in Table 6-1. The Table shows the division and level at which the teams function: A stands for elite, B for developing and C for getting started.

TABLE 6-1
The East, Central, West Division Clubs

Division	Level	Division	Level
EAST		**CENTRAL** (Cont't)	
Atlanta Kookaburras	A	Cincinnati Dockers	A
Baltimore/Washington	A	Detroit Overdrive	C
Boston	A	Kansas City Power	A
Buffalo	C	Louisville Cats	A
Florida	C	Milwaukee Bombers	A
Lehigh Valley Crocodiles	A	Minnesota Freeze	C
		Nashville Kangaroos	A
New York Magpies	A	Austin Crows	B
North Carolina Tigers	A	St. Louis Blues	A
Philadelphia Crows	A	**WEST**	
South Carolina Hawks	C	Denver Bulldogs	
TriCity Saints	A	Los Angeles Crows	A
Vermont	C	Orange County Bombers	A
West Pennsylvania Wallabies	A	Oregon	C
CENTRAL	A	Phoenix Scorpions	A
Chicago Sharks	A	San Diego Lions	A
Chicago Swans	A	Santa Cruz Roos	A
Dallas Magpies	A	Seattle Cats	A

The recently completed championships in Kansas City in October 2002 reflect the format of the National Championships through a process of elimination.

We have included John "Pop" Meier's colorful report in Toto. It reveals the human side of events alongside the intensity of the competition itself.

NATIONAL TOURNAMENT REPORT – 2002
By John "Pops" Meier

Entering the hotel Westin, I was greeted with the loud and boisterous laughter I have come to recognize as footy related. The thumping of a football on the marble floor in the vast and elegant lobby may have sounded out of place to some (namely the nervous manager), however I knew I was undoubtedly in the right place. I managed to pick out a dozen or so of my footy mates I've come to know over the past 3 years.

Yep, this was going to be an unforgettable weekend.

I settled into my room on the 6th floor of the Westin, with a view of magnificent proportion. The roof repair going on next door was breathtakingly intriguing; however, it was the abundance of trees and greenery in the landscape which caught my attention. Remember that I'm from Arizona. I believe we're down to six trees at last count.

Wandering down to the lobby, I found my way into the mezzanine area where the Cooper's Pale Ale was flowing and players from every corner of the US were wolfing meat pies down. Meat pies, eh? Fascinating culinary event these are. I don't get the Vegemite enthusiasm either, but give me time; I'm sure to catch on. I'll bet most Aussies were aghast when at first they were confronted by Jack in the Box tacos or White Castle Sliders.

Relegated for the next four or five hours at the registration desk gave me the opportunity to see many of the arriving players I knew and many of whom were about to become my friends and teammates.

Over 500 players representing 24 different clubs (there were actually 22 teams since two of the teams were combined clubs; Cincinnati/Western PA and Lehigh Valley/Phoenix) crowded into the Westin Crown Center Hotel. Thirty umpires and more than 75 volunteers and officials were also part of this annual event.

The first day of competition began at 8 am at the three lush fields the Kansas City Power Football Club had secured for the weekend of footy. Aside from a spot or two of mud on field 1, the overnight rain had little effect. The nippy 38-degree starting temperature was a bit chilly, but the players, with winning a football match on their mind, eagerly took to the grounds. Field 2 had a little more mud slowing the play down a bit but gave a bit more when a good hip and shoulder sent players sprawling. It also made old slow guys like me look like I could keep up with the young agile players, for about a minute.

The first round of matches chased the dew off the field and the players and level of play began to hit its stride. The skill and competitiveness of the combatants became apparent to those in attendance. In Division 1 play, Nashville, Denver, New York and reigning National champ San Diego dominated their first round opponents. In Division 2 the scores were much closer with Orange County and Dallas edging their opponents, Santa Cruz and St. Louis playing to a tie and Phoenix/Lehigh Valley coming from behind for their first win. Division 3 play was wild with Milwaukee trouncing the New York B squad, Philadelphia doing the same to their opponent. North Carolina edged the Chicago Sharks and the Sharks in turn doing the same the New York B club.

The strikingly sharp level of football was commented upon by many of the spectators who, without question, knew quality football when they saw it while they enjoyed the gorgeous Kansas City weather. Screaming marks and flawless passages of play caused "oohs" and "ahs" from the seasoned spectators. I can only assume those watching players other than me were impressed as well.

At the end of the first day of matches Division 1, the west coast footy machine that is San Diego and Doggies of Denver, seemed to be steamrolling their way to a Grand Final match up. However, New York and Nashville were still to be reckoned with and were close on the heels of the two past champs. Division 2 was less of a predictable race with Lehigh/Phoenix, Santa Cruz, Dallas and Orange County each looking like they could lay claim to the Division 2 championship. Division 3 play found the Tigers of North Carolina and Milwaukee Bombers in position to meet in the championship match for their division.

All in all, at the end of a great first day of matches, nothing was decided for sure, great plays and players were made and everyone knew that each club's performance in the Sunday matches would be crucial to the outcome of the tournament.

But now there was beer to drink and barbecue to be devoured.

The Saturday evening festivities took place in the massive Union Station building. Obviously designed and built about the time of the Pharaohs, hundreds of players and supporters filled the grand hall. The gathering of the tournament participants, always a popular event, showcased the world famous KC barbecue combined with bottles of Cooper's beer. Each attending team certainly did their best to rid the party of both.

At an opportune time, several speeches were made, members of the 2002 Revo squad were presented and the newly elected USAFL board was introduced. At least that was what I thought. There was an acoustic issue in the building. Nevertheless, the whole affair was well done by the KC folks. No one left hungry, that's for sure.

The Sunday morning matches began with a bit of frost on the ground and fog in the air, deciding who would be playing for the divisional Grand Finals. The heat of battle among the clubs was enough to drive the chill from the air. Good thing too, since the alternative would have been to decide the winners by boat races or eating contests. The players scheduled for the 8 am matches were decidedly groggy due to the 3 am FALSE fire alarm rousing slumbering players from their beds and causing a ruckus when at least one player, in his lethargic confusion, mistook the Westin pool for his assigned room and crashed on a sofa in less than usual night clothing.

Philadelphia and Milwaukee narrowly dispatched the Tigers of NC and Sharks of Chicago in the D3 prelims setting the stage for a Grand Final rematch. The Dallas Magpies ran out on the combined team of Cincinnati/Western PA with a 20-point win to earn a 3rd place finish in the D2 race. Santa Cruz blah, blah, blah against Lehigh Valley/Phoenix, blah, blah, blah. The SC Roos blah, blah, blah goals and marks blah, blah, blah for one of the D2 Grand Final berths.

Okay, the Santa Cruz boys took us apart in the early Sunday morning match. With flawless passing and strong marks, the Roos marched up and down the grounds running out a 32-point victory against the combined team now known as the Scorpadiles. Orange County, as expected, put

together another fine performance besting the Swans of Chicago by a margin of 48-9 and taking the final spot in the D2 granny.

The 2001 National Champion and 2002 Champion San Diego Lions continued their march towards repeating as National Champions with an 8-point victory over the New York Magpies in a hotly contested match. The Denver Bulldogs continued their dominance of the D1 pool A by routing the strong Nashville boys, who up to that time had looked like a certain and formidable obstacle in Denver's path.

The rematch between Philly and Milly was fast and furious, though a low scoring affair. Solid defense by the Crows combined with relentless pressure by the Philly on-ballers kept the Bombers at bay (Get it? Bombers-bay? Get it? Nevermind). Playing a possession game the Crows found themselves 12-point winners at the final siren of the D3 final.

The Orange County boys started fast and finished strong in their D2 final match against another West Coast team, the Santa Cruz Roos. The OC Bombers put on a clinic with their precision passes and strong marking. Strong open-field running by Mark Seccull and Donnie Lucero set up plays by Captain David Thurmond and Marty Curry. As long as Marty could keep running, he was sure to kick a goal. The moment he stops...A huge mark just outside the goal square by Bomber Paul Wiggins was, in this writer's eyes, "Mark of the Tourney" as he climbed the ladder to fetch the pill out of the sky.

I would have voted for another strong mark by a teammate who shall remain nameless but he shanked the absolute sitter out on the full from 15 meters out while Paulie dropped the ball to his boot and shot it clean and true for six.

In the end, the Bombers of Orange County ran out winners by a score of 7.3.45 to 2.3.15 over the Santa Cruz boys. The match was full of great plays and excitement and a tremendous curtain raiser to the Div. 1 Grand Final between Denver and defending champion San Diego.

The Denver Bulldogs, strong independents from the heart of the west, were poised to take on the formidable Lions of San Diego. The 4 time CAFL Premiers were looking to dominate the Doggies and lay claim to a repeat championship on the national stage. From the first ruck it was obvious both clubs were determined to be holding the Premier Cup aloft at the end of the day. Early on in the game it was clear the Bulldogs intended to deny the Lions the touches and clear runs we've all become accustomed to seeing the Lion offense utilize while marking the pill strongly in front of the goal. Each loose ball seemed to take a Denver bounce and the Doggies capitalized time and again on even the slightest of miscue by San Diego. Still words of zealous encouragement from Lion's Coach Chris Stiegler couldn't overcome the relentless Denver pressure.

Solid defense and brutal shepherds were delivered by both squads, but still the Denver offense pressed on. Soon however, the chances were becoming fewer and farther in between for the Lions as the gap widened between the two teams. In the end, the entire Denver squad played better to win bragging rights for the second time in three years. For the first time in anyone's memory the Lions were shut out from kicking a six-pointer . The final score was indicative of the enormously effective Bulldog game plan, with the Doggies running out resounding winners 8.1.49 to 0.2.2 to claim the Division 1 2002 USfooty National Championship.

Congratulations to all the players, supporters, officials and volunteers who made the trip. Everyone won just by showing up. It was a great tournament and weekend put on by USfooty and the Kansas City Power Football Club. Newly elected USfooty President Mark Wheeler of Kansas City and his club members are to be commended on a job well done. Great thanks to Andrea Caesar and those at USfooty who worked so hard to make the weekend a success. But now there was beer to drink and barbecue to be devoured.

John Meier, 11/25/2002,

2002 PRESIDENTS REPORT - 2002
By Jon Lenicheck
President 2001-2002

It's hard to believe that the 2002 USAFL season has drawn to a close. In many ways, my life since October, 2001 has felt like a whirlwind. While unfinished business remains for the league and clubs, I can feel good that we are on the path to continued success.

Frankly, the continued explosive growth of the USAFL is startling. To get an idea, take a look at the number of games played in the US. In 1999, 117 games were played – the first time more than 100 games had been played in a single season. By 2001, that had grown to 190, and the question became 'how long until 200 games is no longer a milestone.' At this writing, 196 games are listed as having been played in 2002, and we still have the national tournament to go. It's clear we will reach 200 this season. Now the question becomes, at what point in the 2003 season will we reach 1,000 games, and what two teams will play that historic match.

Why the success? There are a number of factors, I think, but none as important as the dedication of the people involved. While I am most intimately aware of the effort put in by the USAFL Board, the circle is much larger than this. In Santa Cruz, for example, Jeff Finsands has demonstrated a true love for promoting the game to juniors. In Dallas, the Magpies have committed the time and resources to exporting the game to Houston, San Antonio and Austin. In Chicago, Julian Callachor has led the effort to create another regional league, the Lake Michigan Australian Football League. And in North Carolina, Tim Blankenmeyer has organized an ongoing, feisty competition among university clubs in the Research Triangle.

There are many other examples. At the risk of ignoring other specific examples of individuals and clubs promoting the game tirelessly, I will draw myself up short here. Suffice it to say there are many of us Yanks who have joined our ex-pat Australian friends in loving footy. For all of us, no matter where we live or where we grew up, it is for, as my predecessor Rich Mann always liked to say, "for the good of the game."

Lenicheck's Report continues . . . . .

League Growth

The conundrum facing the league as it continues to grow is easy to identify: is growth outpacing our ability to grow? It's a wind sprint for all involved, but I believe the answer is no – growth is not moving more quickly than the league can. However, this is an important footnote to the terrific growth footy has experienced since the 2001 Coopers National Tournament.

It has already been noted that the USAFL is on track to preside over 200 games this year, an all-time high. In addition to the dedication of the people involved, there are indeed other factors for this. One is the addition of new teams, in particular the Chicago Sharks and the Western Pennsylvania Wallabies. Establishing a new club is a combination of hard work and good luck; to my observations, the Sharks and the Wallabies have had plenty of the first and enough of the second. Additionally, the Dallas Magpies have invested significant time into fostering two new clubs in Texas – one in Houston and another based in Austin but also encompassing players from San Antonio. With continued assistance from Dallas, I expect both clubs to come on line as full-fledged USAFL clubs by 2004.

Indirectly related to these new clubs has been the continued growth of regional leagues in the US. While old friends the MAAFL, CAFL and SEAFL returned as strong as ever, two new leagues came on line this year, the North East Australian Football League and the Lake Michigan Australian Football League. Just as the veteran regional leagues have done, it is my belief that these leagues will foster greater competition and will make scheduling easier for individual clubs.

Lastly, it appears that Metro League footy has firmly taken hold. By now, Metro Footy in Arizona may be old news. It shouldn't be. The Arizona Australian Football League has grown to six teams, and also hosted the first ever metro footy tournament in February, 2002, with the Orange County Bombers winning the first ever title. But Metro Footy has grown well beyond the Phoenix metropolitan area. Leagues have grown in Los Angeles (six teams) and Baltimore/Washington DC (four teams). Boston began its own metro competition in August, 2002. Santa Cruz and Denver also have plans to initiate metro leagues.

We have grown so much in 2002, and I anticipate equally positive growth in 2003.

International Game

2002 is a watershed year for the USAFL's involvement in the international aspect of the game for one major reason and several lesser. The 'big deal'? The International Cup in Melbourne played over two weeks in August, 2002. The national team, the American Revolution, had enjoyed success thus far in the international arena. However, this year was the first time we tested America's finest against the best of the rest of the world. The USA emerged from pool play having defeated Samoa, Canada, and the Republic of South Africa, and losing to New Zealand and eventual Cup champion Ireland. In the playoff round, the USA thumped Great Britain to win fifth place. While I could not have predicted this result, I am well pleased with it. By all accounts, the Revolution players acquitted themselves well on and off the field. Kudos to the entire Revolution staff, in particular Head Coach Denis Ryan. While I would not want to endorse unrealistic expectations for the next International Cup in 2005…well, let's just say I expect no worse than fourth place next time.

Looking ahead, I am excited by the possibilities presented by several programs. First, the US will host the Canadian National Team, the Northwind, in 2003. The USAFL has enjoyed a friendly competition with our neighbors to the north, and we look forward to welcoming them back to U.S. soil. Second, in 2004 the Atlantic Alliance Cup will be held on this side of the Atlantic Ocean. I look forward to putting on a good show for our international friends in each of the next two years. Thirdly, the USAFL is moving ahead with plans to form a U23 team to compete in the 2003 Arafura Games in Darwin. This is a calculated risk, and the league is aware of that. The number of under 23 footy players in the States is small; the trip is expensive; it coincides with the end of the academic year for many American universities. Frankly, this venture could fall flat on its face. That is a risk we should all be willing to take. After all, nothing ventured, nothing gained, yes? Lastly, the USAFL has established a relationship with Macquarie University in Sydney for a Macquarie University Scholarship player. One lucky Yank will qualify to study at Macquarie for a semester with free tuition, and train with the university's football club, the Kookaburras.

Revenue Opportunities

Before discussing new revenue opportunities for the league, it's appropriate to acknowledge the continued support of our sponsors from years past, in particular Coopers and Burley Sekem. As well, although not, strictly speaking, a revenue opportunity, it's also appropriate to acknowledge Australian Products, which is in its first year as a supporter of the league.

The single most significant piece of news for the USAFL in 2002 may be that the league was granted 501(C)(3) status by the Internal Revenue Service. In simplest terms, this means that the league is now legally a charitable, non-profit entity. While the number of regulations associated with this is significant, even at times daunting, there are three important aspects to this ruling. First, with a few exceptions, the league does not pay taxes. Second, donations to the league may now qualify for tax write offs for the individual or company making the donation. Third, the league has the opportunity to apply for group exemption. This would allow member clubs of the league to also enjoy the advantages of being a 501(C)(3) institution – as well as the responsibilities, of course.

There are two other noteworthy new revenue opportunities for the league, the USfooty store and a partnership with Acclaim Entertainment. Usfootystore, which may be accessed easily from the USfooty website, represents the league's first attempt to use the internet for direct revenue purposes. Log on to the footy store, and you'll be able to purchase footies, USfooty hats and clothing, even make a donation to the national team, the American Revolution. In time, it is my plan that in the future web surfers will also be able to purchase USAFL club merchandise on USfootystore. Beginning in the late summer, you were able to purchase Acclaim Entertainment's AFL Live 03, for PC or Playstation. This groundbreaking partnership between the USAFL and Acclaim promises to provide the league a steady source of income.

Continued AFL Support

Of course, no President's Report is complete without specifically acknowledging the support and assistance the AFL has offered, not just this year but since the inception of the league. Perhaps many people may only consider the AFL with regards to dollars, but that is not an entirely accurate picture. Thanks to the efforts of numerous people at the AFL, a list including but not limited to Dr. Ross Smith and Mr. Ed Biggs, the USAFL once again has enjoyed support in putting together the USAFL player and umpire scholarships, increased recognition internationally and assistance in bringing the American Revolution to Australia for the International Cup. I look forward to a continued warm and symbiotic relationship with the AFL.

USAFL Board Make Up

One of the most significant moments in the brief history of the USAFL took place last October, at the 2001 Annual General Meeting. It managed to slip by without much fanfare, which is perhaps as instructive as to the maturity of the league as anything else.

At the 2001 AGM, the USAFL's next generation of leadership began to emerge. Stepping down were long time Executive Board members Cameron Murray, Sue Weeks, Rich Mann and Sheri Archer. Within several months of the AGM, two more long-time Board members resigned – Michael Gardiner and Todd MacIntosh.

The 2002 Board's composition is far different than its predecessors. There are more Yanks than ever before on the Board. Clubs which have never sent members to the national governance level have done so for the first time. For anyone still needing a sign that the league has become a permanent fixture, you need look no further than this.

Jon Lenicheck
Presidents Report
11/25/2002

President Mark Wheeler's, President elect for 2003-2004, has written the following words as he takes up the office for the coming year, 2003.

PRESIDENTS INCOMING ADDRESS
By Mark Wheeler
President USAFL 2002-2003

I would like to take the time to thank the outgoing 2002 USAFL board.

I think that the way the 2002 season was handled showed great leadership within a small group of people that bonded very well. Their dedication and time can't be shown here in words, but we all know that it was a mammoth effort from all.

With new blood entering the board, we feel that 2003 will again be another huge year. In 2003 we will see the introduction of "Auskick", lead by Denis Ryan and team, two different scholarship programs to play football in Australia, and a continuing search for new ways to promote the league to the media.

The new USAFL board again will continue to strive forward in continuing to promote and grow footy here in the United States. Again, we will be searching for new sponsors and better ways to implement our structure, so all clubs can continue to grow and we can move from strength to strength.

For all that don't know me; I am an Australian born one-eyed "Tigers" supporter with huge passion about Aussie Football. I started playing when I was six and have only taken time off for some injuries and to spend time as a VFL umpire. I will continue to be the straight talking person that you all know, and will try to continue to bring my passion of football into my new role as President. I play footy with my heart on my sleeve and will bring that passion into my role, and feel with the team I have with me we will have a boomer year. With over 25 years of Football under my belt, at all levels of competition and administration, I feel confident that the knowledge I have will be used wisely.

With the support of the board and clubs, I feel that we can move forward again into 2003 in growth, sponsorship and another game breaking year.

Please join me in welcoming the new board. I urge you to contact the

Vice President for your region with any ideas that you may have. Good luck for all clubs in the upcoming season.

    East VP – Tim Blankemeyer
    Central VP – Jim Martin
    West VP – John "Pops" Meier
    Secretary – Brad Rinklin
    Treasurer – Chris Adams
    Member At Large – Ryan Richardson

Mark "Wheels" Wheeler
President USAFL
12/2/2002

THE STORY OF USfooty

Chapter 7

THE REVOLUTION

The rapid expansion of clubs, interested players and spectators of USfooty led to the concept of a National Team. This the pioneers named the "American Revolution." The presence of burgeoning nations adopting Australian Football enabled the young Americans to find international competition and to take motivation levels to new heights. The Revolution is a team of American youngsters who are playing for home clubs and who have paid their dues and registered with the USAFL in what is called a "Country of Origin" competition. This Chapter deals with the story of a team that began playing friendly games against the Toronto area in Canada, expanded to an inaugural five-nation Atlantic Alliance Cup in London and, finally, participated in the first International Competition in Melbourne, Australia, under the auspices of the AFL in August 2002. It is an ambitious development but one that is now buoyed by international enthusiasm. Fellow author, Greg Narleski, played in London in the five-nation Atlantic Alliance Cup. The coach on that occasion was Dr. Gary Hill.

The first "International" occurred when a team of all comers met in Toronto for a game against the Lawrence Park Rebels. Although not a fully fledged, "International," this game sparked the impetus for USfooty. Players from five US cities comprised this enterprising band that gave rise to the game in the United States. The cities were Cincinnati, Los Angeles, Kansas City, New York and Milwaukee. The first international team was named in 1999 and played in Chicago against Canada. Visiting AFL star, Paul Roos, coached this team to a great win setting up intense rivalry with Canada that continues today. In 2001 the Revolution ventured outside the North American Continent to participate in what has now become the Atlantic Alliance Cup. Timing was unfortunate as the U.S. earned a place in the final but had to withdraw due to commitments back in the United States. The U.S. National Championships were scheduled for the same weekend. The U.S. team had acquitted itself well with two wins and two losses losing to Ireland and Denmark. Ireland prevailed in that tournament. The Revolution looked forward in August 2002 to the Inaugural International competition scheduled for Melbourne, Australia. Eleven nations accepted invitations to compete.

The Revolution team is about youth. There are, of course, exceptions. Two 40-year-old players, Rob Beyersdorf and Jim Baldwin were these exceptions in the Atlantic Alliance Cup in the year 2001. For the Melbourne Championship the emphasis was upon team work. After the first training run, everyone knew each others' name and the team experienced that intangible bond that draws people together for the game and in the years to come. Plugger notes: "It sends chills down your spine. The way the team has performed on and off the field, especially in Melbourne, made me proud. They represented USfooty with aplomb and class. There were some players who were selected but were unable to participate in Melbourne. They were John Bacon (Boston Demons), Dan Green (Orange County Bombers), Jeremy Kraus (Cincinnati Dockers), Mike Herstein (San Diego Lions), and Jared Schrieber (Phoenix Scorpions). The Revolution benefited from the contributions of other interested individuals who were present. Alan Nugent was added as a third coach. The runners were: Rich Mann (now living in Australia) and Andrew Boyle from Portland, Oregon. Water carriers were Bruce Bedfuss and Paul Raisanen from the Milwaukee Bombers. Each team was required to supply one umpire and the Revolution selection was from the Nashville Kangaroos in the person of Jeff Persson. Trainers were Steve Budrick of the Boston Demons and Kristine Lezark of the Kansas City Power. Equipment Manager was Wayne Calliss of the San Diego Lions and the Office Manager was the indefatigable Andrea Caesar of USfooty with Mark Wilcken as documentarian.

Tryouts for the U.S. team were intense with over 110 players nominating for a position. In three tryouts (Los Angeles, Cincinnati, Boston), the unenviable task of whittling the list down to 30 players with twelve alternates was placed in the hands of the Selection Committee. Head Coach, Denis Ryan, Assistant coach Scotty Nicholas and the indubitable Plugger were the mainstays of the selection team. The final list of 30 players is included in Table 7-1. The Alternates, the Coaching and the Administration staff are listed in Table 7-2. By coincidence Demon Captain and Coach, Allen Nugent, was in Melbourne in August going through the routine of visa headaches, so he was co-opted as a third coach.

TABLE 7-1

The Players of American Revolution for 2002 International Cup

Coach: Denis Ryan
Team Manager: Paul O'Keefe

Colors: Royal Blue, Red & White

No.	Name	Club	No.	Name	Club
1	Kevin Fogleman	San Diego Lions	17	Dustin Jones	Lehigh Crocs
2	Chris Olson	Orange County Bombers	18	Dave Thurmond	Orange County Bombers
3	Todd Messenger	Lehigh Crocs	19	Jay Muller	Phoenix Scorpions
4	Pete Ternes	Chicago Swans	20	Josh Loring	Lehigh Crocs
5	Brad Pope	Phoenix Scorpions	21	Matty Dainauski	Denver Bulldogs
6	Charley Ellis	Denver Bulldogs	22	Zach Hollway	Orange County Bombers
7	Jason Amstutz	Orange County Bombers	23	Matt Jagger	St. Louis Blues
8	Heath McDaniel	Boston Demons	24	Chad Martin	Phoenix Scorpions
9	Jeff Purcell	Phoenix Scorpions	25	Josh Loring	Lehigh Crocs
10	Brad Rinklin	Boston Demons	26	BK Gambaro	St. Louis Roos
11	Chris Candelaria	Denver Bulldogs	27	Donovan Trost	San Diego Lions
12	Andy Lindsay	Inland Empire Eagles	28	Kyle Strenski	Milwaukee Bombers
13	Donnie Lucero	Orange County Bombers	30	Lance Van Putten	Nashville Roos
14	Jay Hunter	Baltimore Eagles	43	Marty Curry	Inland Empire Eagles
15	Tommy Ellis	Denver Bulldogs			
16	Jason Becker	Milwaukee Bombers			

Captain, Jeff Purcell; Vice Captains were: Brad Rinklin and Tommy Ellis.

TABLE 7-2

The Alternates, Home Clubs and Coaching Staff of American Revolution For 2002 International Cup

Boston Demons	Greg Narleski and George Lacomy
Chicago Swans	Jeff Fisher
Lehigh Valley Crocs	Mike Zinn
Kansas City Power	Brian Furr
Milwaukee Bombers	Bruce Beilifus
Nashville Kangaroos	Darin Vsetecka
Orange County Bombers	Deran Lean
St. Louis Blues	Jim Martin,
San Diego Lions	Marc Larsen

Head Coach –   Denis Ryan, Baltimore/Washington Eagles
Assistant Coach –   Scott Nicholas, Boston Demons
Co-opted Coach   Alan Nugent, Boston Demons
Head Trainer -   Steve Budrick, Boston Demons
Head of Delegation   Paul O'Keeffe, Milwaukee Bombers

The Revolution arrived in Melbourne on Saturday, August 10, 2002. It was the fourth team assembled under the U.S. flag. Eleven countries sent candidates to this first ever truly international Australian Football Carnival. Previous attempts had been made but were only partially successful. The Arafura Games in Darwin accounted for three assemblies with Papua New Guinea defeating New Zealand in the final on each occasion but the overall entry numbers in this tournament were small. Problems with egos reduced AFL interest in the Arafura Games to a disappointing level. As previously mentioned, the Atlantic Alliance Cup in London in 2001 was diminished when the U.S. team had to go home before the championship finals were played. But the International Cup in Melbourne was to be known as the first serious "Internationals" for Australian football, true "test" matches in the Australian vernacular. The AFL Committee, under Dr. Ross Smith and Ed Biggs, provided competent leadership with the Games being played on AFL and VFL grounds. AFL Clubs in Melbourne hosted generous functions for all teams. The

Organizing Committee decided to stage the round robin competition in two pools with the winners playing a grand final on the MCG as a curtain-raiser to the Hawthorn/Kangaroos game on Friday the 23rd of August. The two pools were: Pool A – Papua New Guinea, Denmark, Great Britain, Japan and Nauru. Pool B consisted of Canada, Ireland, New Zealand, Samoa, South Africa and the U.S.A. Of interest was the ranking which the Committee forecast as the finishing order: (1) Papua New Guinea, (2) New Zealand, (3) Ireland, (4) Denmark, (5) U.S.A. (6) Nauru, (7) Samoa, (8) Great Britain, (9) Canada, (10 Japan, (11) South Africa. These rankings ended up being kind to teams in Pool A which ultimately proved inferior to the teams in Pool B. Ireland carried all before it and won the championship handsomely. It is probably of interest that the Irish team contained a player by the name of David Stynes whose brother Jim was recruited by Ron Barassi in the early 80's and subsequently won a Brownlow Medal competing for Melbourne. Indeed, the Sunday Age on August 11th provided the substance of Table 7-3 which gives the names, countries and Australian clubs of 39 overseas players who have come to Australia and made a success of their football careers.

Table 7-3

Overseas Born VFL/AFL Players

Name	Country Born	Team
Colin Alexander	England	Collingwood/Brisbane
Mark Bayliss	England	Collingwood
Peter Bell	South Korea	Fremantle/North Melbourne
Peter Bennett	New Zealand	Hawthorn/Essendon
Lawrence Bingham	England	Hawthorn/St Kilda
Wayne Blackwell	England	Carlton
Chris Burton	England	Footscray/Richmond
Trent Croad	New Zealand	Hawthorn/Fremantle
Damian Cupido	South Africa	Brisbane
Ian Dargie	England	St Kilda/West Coast
Paul Earley	Ireland	Melbourne
Fred Fairweather	England	North Melbourne
Harry Frei	German	Footscray

Table 7-3 (Continued)
Overseas Born VFL/AFL Players

Name	Country Born	Team
Andy Goodwin	England	Richmond/Melbourne
Milham Hanna	Lebanon	Carlton
Paul Harding	England	Hawthorn/St. Kilda/West Coast
Alex Jesaulenko	Austria	Carlton/St. Kilda
Tadgh Kennelly	Ireland	Sydney
Stephen Lawrence	Zimbabwe	Hawthorn
Johnny Leonard	England	South Melbourne
Stuart Magee	Ireland	South Melbourne/Footscray
John McCarthy	Wales	North Melbourne/Fitzroy
Marty McDonnell	New Zealand	Footscray
Dermott McNichol	Ireland	St. Kilda
Mal Michael	Papua New Guinea	Collingwood/Brisbane
Ian Muller	South Africa	Carlton/St. Kilda
Brian Mynott	England	St. Kilda
Richard Nixon	England	St. Kilda
Tom O'Halloran	New Zealand	South Melbourne
Polly Perkins	England	Richmond
Don Pyke	United States	West Coast
David Rodan	Fiji	Richmond
Jose Romero	Chile	North Melbourne/ Footscray
Wayne Schwass	New Zealand	North Melbourne/Sydney
Joe Sellwood	New Zealand	Geelong
Ben Sexton	New Guinea	Footscray
Jim Stynes	Ireland	Melbourne
Sandford Wheeler	United States	Sydney
Sean Wright	Scotland	Melbourne

The Games were amazing. Understandably, the gap between the best and the worst teams was large. Some countries have only just begun to play the game, others for over 100 years. Papua New Guinea has been playing the game since the days of World War I, and New Zealand has had Australian Football since before the turn of the 20th century. The United States has been active only since 1997 and South Africa began to play footy even later. The South African team consisted of schoolboys, uniformly the size of the Bantu tribesmen. When they played New Zealand they were beaten by 23 goals but it was their first game and they played much better against Canada in the second game. Samoa was beaten by three goals by the U.S.A. but then went on to take Ireland to one goal in their second game. The U.S. finished the tournament in 5th place with four wins and two losses. Their wins were convincing and, unfortunately, their losses were equally convincing. We will discuss each game later in the Chapter. The Games were well covered by radio and television with special features in some of the printing press. <u>The Sun Herald</u>, the <u>Melbourne Age</u>, and the <u>Sunday Age</u> were exceptions. Australian Rules Football's major news organ, <u>The Herald Sun</u>, skirted the Games and did give the results in the scoreboard section, but its coverage was lousy, extremely disappointing, considering the <u>Herald Sun</u>'s history and reputation in covering the game. Individuals in addition to Stynes were reported on with fascination. David Thurmond and Donnie Lucero, from the Orange County Bombers in California, were already in Melbourne playing with Eltham in the Diamond Valley League. A delightful story is told of Donnie when in one game in the U.S. he scored eight goals and a touchdown. A touchdown in Australian Football? Yes, it was his first game; he kicked eight goals and then forgetting which game he was playing raced across the goal line and placed the ball on the ground for a touchdown. Great in Grid Iron, productive in Rugby, yes, but alas it is worth only one point in Australian Football. Footy enthusiast, living in the Gold Coast, Brian Clarke, has another story about a Danish player who jumped high over the pack and headed the ball through the big sticks. Great in soccer, yes, but not in footy. A number of players took advantage of Victorian minor leagues to get some playing time. The surprisingly talented Samoan team placed nine with the Moorrabbin Kangaroos in the Southern Football League. Apparently, the Samoans resolved the problems of accommodation, too, as 29 of them stayed in a four-bedroom house. The pundits picked the Danes as the dark horse, but they were wrong. Nauru was also highly fancied especially as it is the national sport and crowds of 3,000 out of a total population of 10,000 regularly attend their grand final. Jeremy Kraus was the recipient of a three-week training scholarship provided by the Essendon Football Club. Essendon coach, Kevin Sheedy, is a great fan of evangelizing the game throughout the world so it is little wonder that the Cincinnati Dockers youngster was given time to learn much more about the game. He is particularly praising of the goal-kicking tips received from Matthew Lloyd and he actually played in two VFL practice games. "The young American was impressed with the talk on the field." "They go nuts, he said." Kraus plays for the team that was the first National Championship in USfooty back in 1997. Before detailing the Revolution's performance in this eventful enterprise, it is necessary to comment briefly on the progress of Australian Football around the world.

Australian Football Round the Globe

Wayne Jackson, AFL Chief Executive Officer, welcomed the eleven competing teams as pioneers in the first giant leap forwards for Australian Football round the Globe. And he guaranteed continuing AFL support in tentatively scheduling the 2nd and 3rd International Cups for 2005 and 2008. After that, he said, "The tournament could become a four-yearly event." Such world pioneers as Marty Alsford, President of the International Australian Football Council, pioneers Will McKenzie and Brian Clarke and AFL representatives Ross Smith and Ed Biggs were there also to lead the charge. Of course, it is all to no avail unless recognition is also given to those who have started the games in their respective countries. Ex-Demons Champion, Brian Dixon and past U.S. AFL President, Richard Mann, were also very active. These eleven teams from unlikely origins are worth a closer look.

Papua New Guinea (The Mosquitoes)

Papua New Guinea, nicknamed the Mosquitoes, were coached by Andrew Cadzow and managed by Stanley Tavul. The team's colors are black, yellow and red. Footy was introduced to Papua New Guinea as early as the 1930s but particularly in the 1950s by Australian schoolteachers and Defense Force personnel. Regular games were scheduled and permanent clubs were instituted. The AFL's predecessor, the VFL, thought highly enough of the PNG efforts to appoint a full-time manager for their Council. During the 70s, they scheduled games in the Gold Coast, Hobart and Cairns. They won the first gold medal at the 1995 Arafura Games in Darwin defeating New Zealand and played a curtain-raiser to the West Coast/Carlton match in Perth in August 1996. After an important visit by Ed Biggs and Ian Collins, the PNG rules football council drew up a three-year development plan to qualify for financial assistance. Management structures, facilities, improvement and financial estimates were included in this plan. The PNG football team won the next two gold medals, 1997 and 1999, at the Arafura Games again at the expense of the Kiwis. Current coach, Andrew Cadzow, was sent by the AFL as a development officer in the year 2000. Not long after this, the National titles attracted teams from Buka, Pomio, Kove, Hoskins, Kimbe, Lae, Mount Hagen, Port Morseby and Rabaul (what's left of it). Experiments with modified football ensured children were taught the fundamentals of the game. This junior effort is known by the delightful title of Pikinini Pilai Rules. The Papuan New Guineans have been adopted by the Sydney Swans, especially in the form of an annual permanent Kokoda commemoration schedule.

Great Britain (The Bulldogs)

The Footy team from Great Britain is known as the Bulldogs and played in blue, red and white colors. They were coached by Michael Bolt and Martin Tunley, Team Manager was Trevor Wright. The British Australian Football League (BARFL) was formed in May 1990 with eight clubs. They received initial support from the AFL in the form of uniforms and footballs. Four more teams joined by 1992 with the first international matches played against Canada and Hong Kong in 1993. The resilient Greg Everett, currently coach of the Canadian team and Junior Development Officer for U.S. footy, was appointed paid General Manager in early 1994. In 1994 an annual game with Denmark began as a yearly feature with both countries scoring emphatic victories in the first two years. The London Hawks won the premiership from 1993-5; the Wandsworth Demons in 1996 and 1997 and, after losing grand finals in five attempts, the West London Wildcats accounted for their first flag in 2000. Former West Coast, Fitzroy and Brisbane player, Mark Zanotti, arrived in London in 1999 adding his high profile as a great boost to the code especially when appointed CEO. He started new teams and exhibition matches that attracted the attention of the Australian High Commission. In 2001 the BARFL went to a ruling that only 50% of each team could consist of Australians. The British have benefited by having at least one AFL match played at the Oval in London every year since 1986. They performed well in the Alliance Cup in London in 2001 recording wins against Canada and an upset over Denmark.

Nauru (The Chiefs)

The Nauru team is known as the Chiefs. Its colors are navy, with a yellow sash and a white star. They were coached by Gonzaga Namaduk and managed by Valdon Dowiyogo. In this tiny Pacific nation, Australian football is the no. 1 sport. Situated 30 miles south of the Equator, Nauru is divided into 14 districts and has a population of 10,000. Many high profile AFL players and coaches have visited this island. The Nauruans are so crazy about the game that the Christian names of some of the locals are easily recognized: Sheedy, Hawthorn, Jacko, Cazaly, Hudson and Jesaulenko. There are six senior teams in the Nauru Australian Football Association. They have junior and sub-junior competitions as well. Known as the hard men of football, they don't play on grass rather on a phosphate over crushed coral and, despite the lunar appearance, the field markings and posts are identical to those in Australia. Apparently, the game was introduced to Nauruans in the 1930s by schoolboys returning from private education in Victoria. The Leader called the Father of the Nation, Hammer DeRoburt, was a very keen Geelong supporter. The country won the bronze medal at the 1995 Arafura Games. In March of 2000 Nauru's National Team, the Chiefs, won important games against Samoa and a muster of hybrid Australians in Queensland. They repeated this effort a year later. They may never be world beaters but they are capable of nipping the heels of foot-draggers from many other countries.

Japan (The Samurais)

The Japanese team is known as the Samurais. Its colors are red, white and black. The coach was Troy Baird who was assisted by Shane Sibraa and Peter Hosking. Mr. A. W. McLean introduced Australian Football to Japan in 1910. A high school teacher from Melbourne he succeeded in establishing the sport in four large high schools in Tokyo. For the next 80 years the game went into hibernation. In 1986 Hawthorn and Carlton played an exhibition match in Tokyo with the curtain raiser featuring two makeshift teams of Japanese University students. Two of the finest Japanese universities, KEIO and Waseda are arch rivals in everything so they were keen to establish another entity around which they could brawl. The match was the birth of the Japanese Australian Football Association (JAFA). Other universities and expatriates formed a second team to the Samurais called the Goannas in 1991. Today there is a league competition which the various JAFA teams contest regularly. They participated in the Arafura Games in 1995, 1997, 1999 and 2001. Joining the Samurai and Goanna teams are the Gokongs which is a team made up of university graduates and anybody else they can rope in. Japanese firms, such as Panasonic, support these teams.

Denmark (TheVikings)

Not surprisingly the team's popular name is the Vikings with blood red and white as its colors. Coach was Stuart Wynn and team manager Henrick Poulsen. Despite language and distance barriers, Aussie football is flourishing in Denmark. It began in May 1989 with Mark Sitch placing an advertisement in a Copenhagen newspaper asking if anybody would like to meet him under a tree in a public park to kick a footy around. A Dane and a New Zealander turned up which began footy's existence in Denmark. In the 90s three founding clubs, Amager Tigers, the Copenhagen Crocodiles and the North Copenhagen Barracudas were joined by the Aalborg Kangaroos, the Helsingborg Saints, the Farum Cats and the Arhus Bombers. Extensive waterways, myriads of islands, ferries and long bridges make travel difficult. Yet the Danes have negotiated these problems with rare skill. It is interesting to note that Helsingborg is not in Denmark but Sweden, so in a sense the beginnings of footy in Scandinavia are underway. Participation rates are interesting, too: twenty-five percent Australian, 60 percent Danish and Swedish and 15 percent others. The Danes have no difficulty in fielding teams that are known as "State of Origin." The Danish Australian Football League (DAFL) has an ongoing scholarship program with the Victorian Amateur Football Association club, Powerhouse. Every year, at least one Danish player spends time in Melbourne playing and learning the game. Since 1998, a junior program has begun which is destined to further promote the game in Denmark. This central cell in Europe--Ireland, Britain and Denmark--will no doubt expand further onto the Continent bringing Aussie footy closer to the masses.

Canada (The Northwind)

The Canadian Australian Football Association (CAFA) was formed similarly to many U.S. teams. A bunch of Australians drank some beer and kicked the footy around in 1989. Two teams played a game in mid October. Their names were the Toronto Panthers and the Missisauga Mustangs. Not long after, the Scarborough Rebels and the North York Hawks were founded with the Hamilton Wildcats being added to the roster in 1991. Swaps and changes took place in 1992 when the North York

Hawks became the Broadview Hawks and the Balmy Beach Saints were formed. In 1993 the previous year's champions, the Scarborough Rebels, changed site and name to become the Lawrence Park Rebels. Another team, the Brampton Wolverines, was officially declared and the first-ever international series was played against an international team from Great Britain. The Missisauga Mustangs won their first premiership in 1994. In 1995, 21,000 fans saw the Hamilton Wildcats play an All Star Team lineup at the half-time break between two Canadian Football League Teams, Hamilton and Edmonton. The Downtown Dingos were formed in 1996, but the Balmy Beach Saints drowned in a sea of anonymity. In 1998, the competition was strong. However, in 1999 the Brampton Wolverines merged with the Missisauga Mustangs due to falling numbers. In the same year, the Toronto Eagles drew with the Boston Demons in Toronto and a Canadian national team traveled to Chicago to play the U.S.A. Revolution which was reciprocated in the year 2000. The Toronto Dingos reached their first grand final that year. The following year the Vancouver Cougars were formed and played practice games against the Seattle Cats. Western Canada saw encouraging development with the formation of the Edmonton Bush Rangers and the Calgary Kangaroos. In Ontario, the Guelph Gargoyles was founded. The Canadian team, the Northwind, played that same year in the Atlantic Alliance Cup in London and was present for the international competition in Melbourne in August 2002.

Samoa (The Bulldogs)

The Samoan team is known as the Bulldogs. Its colors are royal blue, red and white. The team was coached by Mataieo Simeti and managed by Tupai Avele. This new game in town resulted from a meeting in 1998 in the Samoan capital of Apia. Led by Scott Reid, a group of enthusiasts staged an exhibition match during the cultural festival in September of that year. Misa Sofara described the proceedings in the local language which entertained all and sundry. Two high schools provided the players with the game being umpired by two ANZ Bank employees. It spread rapidly, culminating in six teams within the first year. Simply called Samoan Rules, the teams began with 15 players neatly divided as five forwards, five backs and five on-ballers. The center line was marked on the pitch with the forwards and backs required to stay in their half of the field. And to encourage kicking, players were restricted to one ball bounce only while running. Eight schools joined the fray in 1999. The national team played in the Arafura Games in Darwin in 2000, winning a bronze medal for its efforts. The Western Bulldogs provided the gear and it was not long before the team began to visit other parts of the world. Dermott Brereton interrupted a surfing holiday in Samoa to conduct a training session in November, 1999, which was thoroughly appreciated by all. The next year, a junior team competed in the Jim Stynes trophy in Canberra while two Samoans excelled by playing for Queanbeyan in the Canberra League. Apparently, many Samoans live in New Zealand and are playing in that country's footy teams as well. The Samoan team competed with distinction in the International Cup improving with every game. They pushed Ireland to a point where victory was possible into the last quarter.

New Zealand (The Falcons)

The New Zealand team is known as the Falcons. Its impressive guernseys are colored black with a grey fern on the front. This follows the national motto of the All Blacks. The team was coached by Rod Shaw and managed by Avan Polo. Australian football has a long history in New Zealand. Games are reported as featuring from the 1880s through the start of World War I. Indeed there were 44 teams in 1893 and 115 in 1901. In 1908, New Zealand competed in an Australian football carnival with games played at the MCG, losing to Victoria and Tasmania but defeating NSW and Queensland to finish fourth. A particularly serious difference appeared after 1911 with the parochial Victorian Football League causing a forty-year hiatus in footy's development. It was revived in the 1970s with competitions established in Auckland, Wellington and Christchurch. New Zealand competed three times in the Arafura Games in Darwin, unfortunately losing the grand final each time to Papua New Guinea. These three losses, 1995, 1997, 1999, did not preclude the setting up of a three-year agreement with the AFL to develop football in the land of the Kiwis. Television coverage was provided and investments of AUS$100,000 a year for a three-year period were provided by the AFL. The plan was ambitious, especially at the junior level, and the quality of play improved dramatically. In 1998 Melbourne defeated Sydney before an enthusiastic crowd of 8,000 people at the Basin Reserve in Wellington. Soon games in 2000 and 2001 between the Western Bulldogs and Hawthorn and Brisbane and Adelaide, respectively, created great interest. An under 21 team toured Australia in 2001 winning two of its five matches. This history has been long but sporadic. New Zealand is now set to provide serious competitive aegis to Australian footy and will, we are sure, rapidly contribute to the quality of the sport as they have done in Rugby, Netball, Track and Field, and Sailing.

South Africa (The Buffaloes)

This team is known as the Buffaloes, with jade, red and yellow colors adorning splendid attire which made the South Africans welcome guests at the International Cup. The team was coached by Reggie Mokotedi and managed by Neels Roodt. The South Africans describe Australian Football as the harbinger of exciting times ahead. Their history goes back to the 1890s when Australian miners working in the Transvaal organized a virile competition. The game was played in South Africa during the Boer War by the Australian soldiers with some Australians moving to South Africa believing there was a good future for the game in that country. Unfortunately, as with so many recreational pastimes at that time, the competition stalled around 1905 and died at the beginning of World War I. The long leap forward to 1997 occurred before the game rekindled in the Northwest province of South Africa. A few boxers taking part in the Arafura Games in Darwin were agreeably impressed with the sport. When they returned, they infiltrated the Department of Arts, Culture and Sport in all provinces causing the game to bud out in the newly aligned South African states. An army major, Marty Alsford, began coaching clinics and coined the phrase, "the new sport for the new South Africa." Just five months later in February, 1998, Brisbane defeated Fremantle in an exhibition game before an enthusiastic crowd of 10,000 people. World-renowned Archbishop, Desmond Tutu, tossed the coin to start the game. He was so enthused that he participated in football clinics with children from the surrounding townships. The AFL kicked in with jumpers, shorts, socks and a ball to help the townships gain participatory resolution. In 1998 South Africa competed in Canberra at the Jim Stynes Cup and in 2001 the AFL sent a developmental officer to Mafeking to begin organizing school competitions. Renowned Melbourne champion, Brian Dixon, visited during a Sport-For-All conference and assisted the locals in raising $30,000 to send a team to the International Cup.

Ireland

As yet the Irish have not adopted a nickname but this team will struggle to avoid one if its victories continue to pile up. Not surprisingly, the team colors are light green with a dark green trim. The coach was Darren Fitzpatrick and it was managed by Damien Cassidy. Australian

Football in Ireland has been greatly helped by the visits from League teams with modified rules begun by Ron Barassi in the 80s and continued to this day. The official league was founded in October 2000 when a grand final was played between the Dublin Demons and the Belfast Redbacks. The two clubs played challenge matches with British clubs and actually joined in their competition during preseason games. The Irish performed splendidly finishing third out of 12 teams in their first ever competitive games. Michael Currane, current President and Chief Executive Officer, and Vice President, Ciaran O'Headhra began to promote a league consisting of five clubs. By 2001 this league had two major domestic competitions. One played as a nine-a-side competition enabling it to fit into Gaelic Football field dimensions which made for cheaper and more easily managed schedules and competition. Originally, the senior leagues consisted of 14 members and the Irish were successful in 2001 in winning the Atlantic Alliance Cup in London. They inaugurated a Fosters Aussie Rules Australia Day Challenge Cup on January 26th, 2002. They headed Aussie footy in the right direction that day by staging a special children's program called, "Outonthetown."

The U.S.A. (The Revolution)

The American Revolution sports the colors royal blue, red and white. The team was coached by Denis Ryan, and assisted by Scot Nicholas and Allen Nugent. The team manager was the indefatigable Plugger O'Keeffe. As this book details the story of USfooty, there is no need for a formal introduction. Rather the games played will be discussed with comments and conclusions included.

Games Played

Game 1 - U.S. vs. Samoa

The team's first game in the International Cup was against Samoa on Wednesday, August 14 at Sandringham's ground on Port Phillip Bay. It had rained heavily for two days and it was cold. The Revolution was without Vice Captain, Brad Rinklin of the Boston Demons, due to a bout of pancreatitis landing him in hospital for two days. The ball was slippery and the weather cold for the 10 am start. Four 15-minute quarters were played which was standard procedure for all the games including the grand final. The Revolution coaches avoided tripping over one another by taking responsibility for coaching in the following ways: Denis Ryan took the forwards, Scotty Nicholas the backs and Alan Nugent the rucks and rovers. Each would address their constituencies, then Ryan would deliver a closing speech intended to inspire his charges. From first-hand information the advice seemed good. Channels 9, 10 and 7 were there to record the start of the game as was Channel 31 which is a minor station in the Melbourne area. Each team lined up in a hollow square with the referees connecting the teams. Both national anthems were played with the Samoans adding color by doing their version of the Haka. It was colorful and appreciated. Chad Martin from the Phoenix Scorpions was outstanding in the first quarter, but in the poor conditions the U.S. handled the ball uncertainly. Jason Becker, from Milwaukee, scored the first goal in International Cup history, surely a sports trivia question for the ages. At quarter time the score was tied 2-2 a piece. For a time in the second quarter, the Samoans dominated kicking the first goal and playing with great zest. Although the conditions were still slippery, the sun was working to dry up the ground as both sides tackled fiercely. The U.S. disposal was blind, and time and again the backs cleared the ball only to be intercepted. The U.S. began to prevail and finished leading at half time 4.4 to 2.6. During the third quarter the gallant Samoans kicked the first goal but faded at this time. The U.S. started the fourth quarter 6.5 to 3.7 and, after some strong marking, went onto win 7.9 to 4.8. The rankings expected the U.S. to win. They were ranked fifth and Samoa seventh, but the Samoans played courageously and went on to greatly improved efforts later on in the tournament. It was a critical win for United States.

Game 2 – U.S. vs. New Zealand

At 2 pm on August 15 the Revolution lined up against one of the tournament favorites, New Zealand, on the renowned Port Melbourne Football Ground. The Revolution supporters were horrified to see the team proliferate into hurried small kicks which usually ended up in a pair of Kiwi hands. The U.S. team was out marked, out thought and failed to penetrate the half-back line of the Falcons. The Kiwis led 3.1 to 1.1 at the beginning of the second quarter. It was painful to watch the second quarter as New Zealand were playing in front using better handball and talking intelligently to each other. The Revolution dissipated into individualized play and refused to go straight down the ground to goal for most of the quarter. It didn't help that they were one man short for 10 minutes due to an unnecessary infringement which brought on a yellow card to a Revolution player. New Zealand led 9.7 to 3.1 at the beginning of the last quarter. The Revolution was a little unlucky in receiving a second yellow card which did not help its cause. The team played much better in the last quarter finishing the game, New Zealand 11.11 to the Revolution 4.1. It was an object lesson in playing the Australian game giving cause for reflection and thought to coaches and players for the kinds of skills needed to win an International Cup. Far too many Revolution players took their eyes off the ball and concentrated on the man when the clashes developed. Far too many balls were kicked sideways instead of through the goals, which is the way to win any football game. This disease exacerbated by such statistics as numbers of possessions perpetrated in the media an unfortunate blight which has entered the game in recent years. Accurate kicking sideways to a man who has made position and who can then drive the ball long to advantage is fine but tapping a ball sideways, even backwards, to contested teammates is a recipe for disaster. Old timers watching in the stands gasped their breath audibly as they saw this weakness continuously unfold. "Kick the bloody ball!" was a phrase heard many times during the conduct of the first International Cup.

Game 3 – U.S. vs. Ireland

This game was played in Geelong on Saturday, 17th of August. Although the sun shone obligingly, the atmosphere was brisk. It was 1 o'clock and the Revolution lined up against the winners of the Atlantic Alliance Cup in London on the old Kardinia Park now renamed Skilled Stadium. The Revolution started the first quarter kicking with the wind but was slow to move the ball and was haphazard in defending against good opponent marking. The players' lack of football know-how was demonstrated in this game more than any other they played. The knack of knowing where the ball would go is an attribute learned only after long participation over many years and the Revolution was continuously caught out of position with dire circumstances. At quarter time, the Irish led 3.1 to 1.1. At half time, the Irish led 5.4 to the Revolution's 2.1. This was the most disappointing quarter of football the Revolution put in during the Carnival. Their efforts were "soft" allowing opponents to run unimpeded all over the ground. It was interesting to hear one spectator offer an excuse for Irish resilience. "You know one third of the team comes from County Cork and they just love popping things out all over the ground." In the third quarter the Revolution played much better, apparently ashamed of their first half. They wanted the ball, began kicking much straighter and finished still in the game at 6.6 to 5.7. During the last quarter they again lifted their play to finish the game a disappointing 10 points behind the Irish. Final scores were 7.7 to 6.3. All three coaches expressed the feeling that this was the team's most disappointing performance. With a better first half the U.S. could have defeated Ireland. Its efforts, however, could be described in those fateful words of "too little too late."

Game 4 – U.S. vs. Canada

The fourth game saw the U.S. matched against its perennial foe, Canada, at Elsternwick Park on Monday, August 19. They have always enjoyed strong competition with their northern neighbors but on this occasion proved far too strong. They led Canada 2.1 to 0 score at quarter time and finished the game 8.4 to 1.1 running away with the game in the last quarter. Greg Everett, the Canadian coach, worked furiously to boost his team but they failed to respond. The U.S.A., on the other hand, played well. Finally, using a more direct approach to goal, with good teamwork, intelligent talk and attacking handball, the team did much to erase the memories of their losses against New Zealand and Ireland. It is interesting to note that the Samoan team took Ireland to one goal in the second round and easily accounted for South Africa in round three.

Game 5 – U.S. vs. South Africa

The team returned to the Port Melbourne ground on Wednesday, 21st August to play its final round-robin performance against the courageous but vastly undermanned South African team. It was a beautiful sunny day. The U.S. led by four goals at the first turn, seven at half time, fourteen at three-quarter time and ran out winners 20.12 to four points. The South African team consisted of schoolboys from tribes like the Bantus. They were constantly outgunned, outmarked and outplayed. The game was unfortunate in that it became so one-sided but losses like this are important to teams when they plan for the future. They know where they stand. It is very likely by the year 2005 that South Africa will be a vastly different foe. The U.S., on the other hand, benefited from continuing practice in the basic skills of this game. Their talk was more directed; they tackled fiercely for the ball and handballed out of packs to advantage. They marked well and kicked straight. Their coaches' directions now more readily matched the terms of their play. The longer the tournament went, the better the Americans performed.

Ireland upset the favored New Zealand on that same day setting up a grand final between the Pool B champions and those of Pool A, Papua New Guinea. The New Zealanders lapsed badly during this game eventually dropping their ranking from second to third when the finals were played to determine the overall International Cup places.

Interpool Final

Game 6 – U.S. vs. Great Britain

The U.S. played Great Britain on the famous junction oval in St. Kilda at 2 pm on Friday 23rd of August. It was playing for fifth and sixth positions. The team was addressed by Ron Barassi after this game which was won conclusively by the U.S.A. 13 goals, 15 behinds to 2 goals, 3 behinds. With mischievous twinkle he suggested that the U.S. was following Australia's example in beating up on the Mother country. This paragon of football, especially international football efforts, however, took a moment to assure the team that what they had accomplished these past two weeks was in the best interests of the game. "We must build an ethic of good sportsmanship and teamwork ahead of the game's development in the global sense." He likened it to Rugby and wished everyone the best of good fortune. The U.S. team finished the tournament the way it would have wished on Day 1. The U.S. team members played direct football, they backed up, they ran hard, glued their eyes on the ball, and marked beautifully. Their efforts were in direct contrast to the British players whose game fell apart as the day went on. It was the Revolution's second victory against Great Britain following on from its performance in the Atlantic Alliance Cup the previous year. In the back of each Revolution mind lurked an incandescent suspicion, tighter football in the first halves of the games against New Zealand and Ireland could have brought a first ranking to the team from the U.S.A. However, that is football and the task lies ahead for the Revolution who will surely play annual games now leading to the next International Cup competition in 2005 and a bonanza celebrating 150 years of Australian football, in Melbourne, in 2008. Table 7-4 lists the essential statistics of the series.

TABLE 7-4
Goal Kickers and Best Players for U.S. Games
In 2002 International Cup

Round 1 – U.S.A. vs. Samoa
   USA – 7-10, 52
   Samoa – 4-7, 31

	Goal Kickers:	Peter Ternes	3
		Jason Becker –	2
		Jon Loring	1
		Marty Curry	1

   Best on the Ground   Chad Martin, Jon Loring, Peter Ternes
                        Charley Ellis, Marty Curry

Round 2 – U.S.A. vs. New Zealand
   NZ – 11-12, 78
   USA – 4-1, 25

   Goal Kickers   Peter Ternes   2
                   Matty Dainauski   1
                   Jeff Purcell   1

   Best on the Ground   Donnie Lucero, Chad Martin, Charley Ellis,
                        Jason Amstutz, Jon Loring

Round 3 – U.S.A. vs. Ireland
   Ireland 7-7, 49
   USA 6-3, 39

   Goal Kickers   Peter Ternes,
                   Dave Thurmond
                   Bradley Rinklin
                   Matty Danauski
                   Dustin Jones
                   Jeff Purcell

TABLE 7-4 (Continued)
Goal Kickers and Best Players for U.S. Games In 2002 International Cup

Best on the Ground	Charley Ellis, Jon Loring, Dustin Jones, Chad Martin	

Round 4 – U.S.A. vs. Canada
USA – 8-4, 52
Canada – 1-1, 7

Goal Kickers	Peter Ternes	4
	Brad Rinklin	2
	Charlie Ellis	2
Best on the Ground	Chad Martin, Charley Ellis, Donnie Lucero	
	Donovan Trost, Matt Jagger, Zach Holway	
	Brad Rinklin	

Round 5 – U.S.A. vs. South Africa
USA – 20-12, 132
SA – 0-4, 4

Goal Kickers	Jeff Purcell	8
	Marty Curry	3
	Matty Dainauski	2
	Lance Van Putten	2
	Heath McDaniel	1
	Peter Ternes	1
	Dustin Jones	1
	Charley Ellis	1
	Todd Messenger	1
Best on the Ground	Tommy Ellis, Matt Jagger, Heath McDaniel	
	Jeff Purcell, Todd Messenger, J. Hunter	

Interpool – U.S.A. vs. Great Britain
USA – 13-15, 93
GB – 2-3, 15

Goal Kickers	Peter Ternes	6
	Jeff Purcell	2
	Jay Hunter	2
	Brad Pope	1
	Charles Ellis	1
	Brad Rinklin	1

Best on the Ground Peter Ternes, Chad Martin, Donovan Trost, Jon Loring, Brad Rinklin, Jeff Purcell

The first International competition was sufficiently successful to warrant the Organizing Committee sending out notes of recognition to the following people. The list is quietly impressive and the report of Ed Biggs is also revealing.

INTERNATIONAL CUP 2002

14-23 August - Melbourne, Australia

APPRECIATION

Organizing Committee

Paul Milo
Will McKenzie
Brian Clarke
Brian Dixon
Matt Glynn

AFL International Development Committee

Valdon Dowlyogo
Claran O'Hara
Richard Mann
Marty Alsford
Roger Ley

Competition Umpiring Manager   Neville Nash

Team Managers

Canada - Sherelle Kelly
Denmark - Henrik Poulson

Great Britain - Trevor Wright
Ireland - Damien Cassidy
Japan - Simon Evans
Nauru - Valdon Dowiyogo

New Zealand - Avan Polo
Papua New Guinea - Stanley Tavul
Samoa - Tupai Avele
South Africa - Neels Roodt
USA - Paul O'Keeffe

Venue Managers

Elsternwick Park - Phil Stevens
Trevor Barker Oval - John Mennie
Skilled Stadium – Quintin Gleeson
Warrawee Park - Rob Oliver

TEAC Oval - Barry Kidd
Junction Oval - Peter Roach
Victoria - Cameron Howell
Whitten Oval - Paul Armstrong

Sports Trainers

Garry Bilson
Glenys Browne

St John's Ambulance

International Cup 2002
Ed Bigg's Report

By any measure the inaugural Australian Football International Cup was an outstanding success, clearly exceeding expectations.

The attendance of 11 teams from countries around the world, each of them responsible for their own travel, accommodation and associated team costs is testimony to the commitment of many voluntary officials to the International Development of our great Australian game. The competition was played in a great spirit, of a standard generally higher than many had anticipated and significantly increased the international profile within

Australian Football circles. The International Cup Dinner held at Colonial Stadium on Wednesday 21 August was a highlight with 400 international visitors joining in a spontaneous cultural exchange with each other and local leading Australian football personalities.

The event was a huge logistical exercise for the Organizing Committee and AFL Administration, requiring the appointment of 120 umpires from Metropolitan Leagues, the use of eight venues, many local volunteers and training staff and a large section of the AFL staff. Planning and preparation took some 18 months for the Organizing Committee and the AFL's International Development Committee.

Congratulations are extended to all teams and participants for their involvement but in particular Ireland for winning the inaugural title, Fia Too Too (Samoa) International Cup Best and Fairest Player, Vince Serci (New Zealand) Leading Goalkicker and Rex Leka (Papua New Guinea) Best Player in Grand Final. Congratulations also to each of the 24 players selected in the International Team.

This inaugural Australian Football International Cup proved to be a true world festival of Australian Football ensuring the ongoing success of the event, with all 11 countries agreeing to participate again in 2005. The following pages record all match results, best players, goalkickers, International Team and acknowledgements for extensive support received in conducting this historic event.

Ed Biggs
Competition Manager
29 August 2002

TABLE 7-5

FINAL PLACINGS

1st	Ireland
2nd	Papua New Guinea
3rd	New Zealand
4th	Denmark
5th	USA
6th	Great Britain
7th	Samoa
8th	Nauru
9th	Canada
10th	Japan
11th	South Africa

AWARDS

Best and Fairest - Fia Too Too (Samoa)

Leading Goal kicker - Vince Serci (New Zealand)

Best Player in Grand Final - Rex Leka (Papua New Guinea)

TABLE 7-6

BEST AND FAIREST VOTES

Player	Country	Votes
Fia Too Too	Samoa	23
Johnny Bosko	Papua New Guinea	18
Vince Serci	New Zealand	17
Aaron Flood	Ireland	15
Navu Maha	Papua New Guinea	15
Mogens Hansen	Denmark	15
Ryan McFlynn	Ireland	15
Mike Seversinsen	New Zealand	15
Henry Simpson	Great Britain	14
Mtutuzeli Hlomela	South Africa	14
Erick Krolmark	Denmark	11
Gary lane	Ireland	10
Quinsen Cook	Nauru	10
Mark Block	Canada	10
Chad Martin	USA	9
Yuta Kobayashi	Japan	9
Marty Curry	USA	9

TABLE 7-7
INTERNATIONAL TEAM

Country	No	Name	Club
Canada	12	Stefan	Broadview Hawks
Denmark	8	Eric Krolmark	North Copenhagen
Denmark	16	Mogens Hansen	North Copenhagen
Great Britain	15	John Boyle	West London
Great Britain	17	Ben Rees	Sussex
Ireland	1	Michael Johnson	Belfast Redbacks
Ireland	3	Aaron Flood	Midland Tigers
Ireland	18	Liam O'Connor	Leeside Lions
Ireland	26	David Stynes	Dublin Demons
Japan	11	Yuta Kobayasi	Goannas
Nauru	1	Alfred Spanner	Menaida
Nauru	9	Quinson Cook	Menaida
New Zealand	18	Vince Serci	Eastern Suburbs
New Zealand	20	Steve Froggatt	University
New Zealand	27	Mike Seversinsen	Eastern Suburbs
Papua New Guinea	1	Walter Yangomina	Enga
Papua New Guinea	5	John Bosko	Morobe
Papua New Guinea	14	Navu Maha	Central
Papua New Guinea	17	Overa Gibson	Gulf
Samoa	15	Fia Too Too	Clayton
Samoa	22	Mika Resamino	Fasitoo-Uta Tigers
South Africa	12	Mtutuzeli Hlomela	Johannesburg
United States	6	Charley Ellis	Denver Bulldogs
United States	24	Chad Martin	Phoenix Scorpions

The Future

Official and unofficial delegates from the eleven countries met on Thursday, 22nd of August, in the spacious rooms of the Carlton Crest Hotel in St Kilda. They were joined by Ross Smith, Ed Biggs and other representatives from the AFL. Present, too, were the executives of the International Football Council (Arafura Games) and the Jim Stynes Trophy (held in Canberra every other year). The very first motion placed before the delegates by the President of the International Football Council (Marty Alsford) and seconded by Will McKenzie, a sterling pioneer from New Zealand, was. "We move that the International Football Council be declared nonexistent," or words to this affect. The vote in favor was unanimous. A sincere disgruntled Arafura Games supporter, Brian Clarke, stood and placed a position before the meeting. This latest move now provided all of the power of running Australian Football in the hands of the AFL. Nobody supported his objection. It was the intention of all to follow a new lead which established a working committee within the AFL to handle the expansion of the game. Although sympathy was expressed to the view that competitive organizations might keep "the bastards honest," cooler heads prevailed and the realization that sponsorship needs, sensible planning and rational development were all needed if this wonderful start was to be given momentum. It must be said, too, that representatives of the AFL conducted themselves with dignity and sincerity. There was not an arrogant position taken during the afternoon proceedings and if this attitude prevails the future for international Australian football is assured.

It is likely that other nations will join the quest. Dr. Rob Hess, a leading sports historian from Victoria University in Melbourne, suggests that the Chinese might also join the growing clan. Apparently, during the 19th century, the Chinese community had players performing with Carlton in 1908 and in the Bendigo League in the 1920s. A group of pig-tailed Chinese miners and gardeners apparently played for a Chinese premiership in Ballarat between 1892 and 1896 and drew crowds of up to 4,000 for that game. Dr. Hess predicts that China one day will throw its considerable population into the Australian Football mix.

Under 23 Team

As 2002 faded the USAFL announced yet another international initiative – the formation of an under 23 team called the "under 23" Revolution or, U23. This team was to journey to Darwin in May 2003 to participate in the Arafura Games. Richard Lozano was named manager. The team selection consisted of:

Baltimore	Nick Cossentino
Orange County	Dan Greene, Andy Lindsey
New York	Adam Mantzaris
Lehigh Valley	Dustin Jones, Todd Messinger, Josh Loring, Jon Loring, Mike Zinne, Dusty Malavolta
North Carolina	Ben Hess, Sam Stern, Phil Schriebman Matt Gordon, Justin Davis
Dallas	Brandon Blackenship
Phoenix	Jon Martinez, R. Boone McGlauglin
St. Louis	Daniel Kocka, Matt Rebstock
Denver	David Kennedy
Pittsburgh	Justin Valley, Mike Colligan
Philadelphia	Tim Weir, Liam McGroarity
Milwaukee	Paul Raisenen, Jared Brunmeier, Aaron Siegal
Cincinnati	Jeremy Kraus
Alternates	Shawn Sadowski (MIL), Noah Koch (LVC), Pat Miller (Phil and Chris McCintry (NY)

Unfortunately, because of the outbreak of infectious disease, Severe Acute Respiratory Syndrome (SARS), the 2003 Carnival had to be abandoned. At the printing of this book, the intent was for the Under-23 concept to continue. A game for 2003 was in the planning stages.

---

[1] P.S. Information for this Chapter has been taken from the International Cup Official Souvenir Program and various press reports from local newspapers and other public media. Our thanks go to the various authors for assembling important information in this regard.

THE STORY OF USfooty

Chapter 8

QUO VADIS

The <u>Melbourne Herald Sun</u> of March 2nd, 2002, tucked away in a minor section of page 10, carried the following article which we will quote in full.

Real Footy in the US

"The war in Afghanistan, George W. Bush at the White House and . . . Aussie Rules." That's what six or seven million Americans watching the ABC prime-time evening news saw last night. ABC reporter Mike Lee and former Bombers ruckman John Barnes showed viewers what AFL was like at its toughest – brawls, shirtfronts, punches and late hits.

"This is football. A different kind of football," Lee explained, marveling at players' toughness and saying the game was the essence of the Australian male."

Over the past five years, the true pioneers of USfooty have striven to present the Australian game as a magnificent struggle of human beings contesting a ball with safe and consistent energies in search of victory. And everybody who has come in contact with this magnificent game has agreed that well-controlled, well-umpired and cooperatively played teams of human beings represent what is arguably the finest game on Mother Earth. Like all games, the seamier side that promotes chauvinism, injury, predatorial aggression and war is introduced by low-life from the garbage heaps of human endeavor. Recent developments in Australia outlawing "kicking in danger," "shirt fronting" and shameful rough-house have been applauded by the US pioneers. It is interesting to note that these acts were outlawed first in the U.S.A. at the 1998 Umpires clinic, in Denver. It was realized and reasoned that the game would spread more easily if predatory nonsense was removed. The American mother eschews her children looking like pretzels instead of human beings as result of youth sport. It is unfortunate that a very small section of the Australian and World press seeks to extract capital from such misrepresentation. The Australian game is not war and is not animalistic chaos as this segment portrayed. And the authors can imagine the frustration the pioneers felt when this performance was brought to their attention. The Australian game is a contact game and some injuries will result, but like all decent human activities the intentions of the contest are for rigor, enjoyment, personal discipline and satisfaction. Where intentions are malignant, the game loses its flavor, its essence and degenerates into something akin to the dreaded "Roller Ball." The intentions, on the other hand, of managers, coaches, umpires, sundry officials, and players are for the game to function with a spirit of enterprise and endeavor that elevates the human spirit rather than decimates humanity.

Parts of the roughhouse tape surfaced again in an episode constructed by well-meaning but ill-informed media specialists during the International Cup in Melbourne in August 2002. The representatives were shown a segment, which included scenes of extreme roughhousing from the 70's along with more current scenes, which could be taken out of context by the viewing public. Revolution coach, Denis Ryan, was filmed during his final address to his team prior to Game 1. Denis, unfortunately, demonstrated his intended motivational ethic by grabbing the sweater of one of the ruckmen mauling him with squeezes and shakes and far from gentle pushes. The resultant howling of the Revolution squad achieved Denis's objective whereby he promptly let his ruckman go, clapped his hands and sent his team sprinting onto the field. When appraised that this incident had been filmed and shown on commercial television, an ashen Denis shook his head and remarked, "Oh, my God, that's the very thing I have preached against for five years." There is a predilection in the unfettered press featuring the belief that roughhouse will improve ratings. The American Professional Football commentators in the bad old days would train the television cameras on every dispute whether it was field or stand. They were shocked when convinced by crowd-behavior experts that people did not appreciate roughhouse segments, especially when presented continuously. The ABC producers for Monday night's football made a conscious decision not to film the brawls but to train back to the commentators during these interludes.

Again, the letters of gratitude, which poured into the station justifying the fan-behavior experts' recommendation, surprised them.

In his 2001 presidential report, outgoing President, Rich Mann, spoke with enthusiasm about all aspects of the development in the United States. With the support, especially of Coopers Brewery of South Australia, MacPherson's Winery, Red Bull and Outback Steakhouse, along with generous provisions of the AFL, the US game is thriving.

The Minutes of the 2001 Annual General Meeting supplied supporting data. Jim Baldwin spoke of junior development with example and enthusiasm. Rob Kelly detailed efforts to attain quality umpires at Level 1 standard and detailed efforts towards Level 2 standards by 2004. The National Tournament, just completed in Baltimore/Washington, was discussed. It was agreed that regions and city size did not matter as much as the excellence of the bids. Kansas City Power obtained permission to run the 2002 National Championships. Later, they were granted permission to run the 2003 National Championships. Sheri Archer and Nashville President, Shane Clohesy, gained agreement that a two-year advance bid process should take place. The motion was passed unanimously. An effort to move the carnival to a three-day format failed. A motion to allow Canadian clubs to participate in the tournament without joining the USAFL failed, but a motion to allow Canadian residents once registered with a U.S. team to play in the National Tournament with an American Club passed. As a matter of interest, a proposal by Canada was presented at the 2003 Administrators Conference in San Diego to move for a four-yearly North American Tournament to be conducted which included Canadian teams was presented. Not only did the motion pass but it was voted on with resounding applause from all clubs. A motion for the USAFL to move towards regional tournaments for seeding purposes passed. A motion to increase team sizes to 18 players was tabled, as was a vote on teams to adhere to the 50% non-Australian rule during the regular season. Women players, provided they are willing to sign a waiver denying special rights, were now permitted to play. In general business, Plugger assured all teams that they were now able to get the 501©(3) tax-exempt status through the USAFL. National sponsorship was accepted but restrictions were not placed on individual club's sponsorship efforts. It was agreed that an administrator's conference similar to that held in Cincinnati in 2001 would be convened in Phoenix in April 2002. Surveys and administrative questionnaires were handed out. The election of office bearers was without surprise.
        Jon Lenicheck, President
        Wayne Calliss, West Vice President
        Todd McIntosh, Central Vice President

Darren Beazley, East Vice President
Ryan Richardson, Treasurer
Chris Adams, Secretary
Paul O'Keeffe, Member at Large

With the loss of Sheri Archer, it was time for the League to employ a full-time employee. Andrea Caesar became the Office Manager. Perhaps it is typical of the progressive thinking of USfooty that it would start its permanent officer drives with a "Caesar." Andrea, who fell in love with football whilst in Australia on her first visit in 1995 took on a host of roles in managing the office. She made the journey to Melbourne with the Revolution for the 2002 International Cup. She never stopped managing, gathering, phoning and generally fulfilling a myriad of organizational missions from dawn to dusk. New President, Jon Lenicheck, the ex Boston President, who works for Federal Congressman, Mike Capuano, in Massachusetts, was ecstatic. Other new members of the Board were Chris Adams, Secretary, and Ryan Richardson, Treasurer. Chris was born in Melbourne but moved to Virginia and earned a Ph.D. in Economics from the University of Wisconsin in Madison. Chris smiles as he details his Australian football experience as limited to the East Ringwood Under 13, Thirds. In the US he played first with the Milwaukee Bombers and then with Baltimore/Washington Eagles. Ryan Richardson played with the St. Louis Blues back in 1997 where he became President but soon after moved to California and played for the Santa Cruz Roos. He holds an MBA and a JD from the University of Missouri, Columbia. The full 2002 board with administrative officers and heads of committees read as follows:

TABLE 8-1

USAFL BOARD 2001-2002

President –	Jon Lenicheck
Secretary	Chris Adams
Treasurer	Ryan Richardson
Executive Director	Sid Caesar
Officer Manager	Andrea Caesar
East Vice President	Darren Beazley and Jeff Farnham
West Vice President	Wayne Callis

TABLE 8-1 (Continued)
USAFL BOARD 2001-2002

Central Vice President	Todd McIntosh, Jim Martin
Webmaster	Matt Muller
Junior Development	Jim Baldwin
North American Junior Strategy	Greg Everett
Umpire Development	Robert Kelly
Umpire Coach	Andrew Boyle
Revolution Coach	Denis Ryan
Coach and Player Development –	Denis Ryan

By October 2002, the full board had developed further with several new positions filled by willing applicants. At the Annual General Meeting held in Kansas City during the National Championships, the following new board for 2003-2004 was elected:

TABLE 8-2
USAFL BOARD 2002-2003

Name	Email
Mark Wheeler, President	President@usfooty.com
John "Pops" Meier, VP – West	Westvp@usfooty.com
Jim Martin, VP – Central	Centralvp@usfooty.com
Tim Blankemeyer, VP – East	Eastvp@usfooty.com
Chris Adams, Treasurer	Treasurer@usfooty.com
Brad Rinklin, Secretary	Secretary@usfooty.com

TABLE 8-2 (Continued)
USAFL BOARD 2002-2003

Name	Email
Andrea Caesar, Office Mgr. 3 Maryland Avenue Rockville, MD 20850-2327	Officemanager@usfooty.com
Ryan Richardson Member-at-large	Memberatlarge@usfooty.com
Robert Kelly Umpire Development	Umpires@usfooty.com
Steve Arnott, Umpire Coach	Umpirescoach@usfooty.com
Jeff Purcell Junior Development	Juniors@usfooty.com
Denis Ryan National Coaching Director	Coachingdirector@usfooty.com
Rob Giabardo, U23 Coach	u23coach@usfooty.com
Rich Lozano, U23 Manager	u23manager@\usfooty.com
Scott Nicholas, Coach & Player Development	Coachingdevelopment@usfooty.com
Scott Hunt, Public Relations	Publicrelations@usfooty.com
Richard Mann, Head of Australian Operations	Australianliaison@usfooty.com
Matt Muller, Webmaster	Webmaster@usfooty.com
Paul O'Keeffe International Liaison	paul@usfooty.com

At the convocation of administrators in Phoenix during the April discussions, the authors sat down with many leading club representatives as well as the National Board and discussed the future of USfooty. It was an exciting time. John Lenicheck's enthusiastic and insightful report is included in Chapter 6.

Perhaps the following centers of concentration will enable the future discussions to undertake some order. Obviously, future possibilities are endless and the juncture USfooty has reached at the end of 2002 was exciting for all those who believe Australian Football is too good a game to be left in the pastures during the 21st century.

1. **Consolidation**

Much discussion both in Cincinnati and Arizona centered on the rules for the various competitions of each year. It is apparent that USfooty will stay very closely tied to the rules of the Mother country with specific attention being paid to reducing the effects of roughhouse. Teams, both in size and structure, were prodigiously discussed. The eligibility factor was keenly debated. Such questions as when is a compatriot not a compatriot, what percentages of expatriates and Americans should be allowed to play, should women be allowed to play and how long must a player have played, or how many games, before he or she is able to play in the nationals or internationals. The schedules are under constant discussion due to financial feasibility and the three types of convocations are under continuous review: (1) the one-off game between typical arch rivals; (2) generic- and legend-building tournaments with old rivals and (3) what form would the Nationals take. Also included in consolidation is the unlovely but essential work associated with the individual clubs and the recruiting especially of American players.

2. **Buildings and Grounds**

American grounds are not suitable for Australian Football like the cricket grounds are throughout the British Commonwealth. There is, of course, ground space, but often season and finance limit its procurement. Most clubs mention difficulties when securing grounds. The competitions have been adapted to suit the restrictions imposed by this problem. The growth of MetroFooty is the future of the game in the U.S.A. This nine-a-side version of the game has been the reason for the second spurt of growth in the sport stateside.

3. **The National Championships**

The original forefathers, most of who are still alive, had the good sense to plan for the National Championships from the outset. This important tradition has given visibility to the teams and a central goal for all the various districts, tournaments, and even one-off games. Something will have to be done about the duration of these championships and the rotation from area to area. Two twenty minute halves are probably not long enough to determine the real strengths of all teams, and the days over which the Nationals are conducted must soon be lengthened from two to four or five. Injuries, squad numbers, and the necessary financial support services are all issues needing to be addressed.

4. **Sponsorships**

The respective boards over the five years of USAFL existence have been quite successful in gaining both commercial and AFL assistance, but these contributions are a mere drop in the bucket of the gut-wrenching quantities which will be needed to propel USfooty into the big time. Any financing efforts will need support by individuals and institutions, major businesses and membership monies contributed by the participants. Frankly, until this problem is alleviated, USfooty will continue as a very minor sport in the U.S.

5. **Media Attention**

Regular reporting in addition to convocational assemblies must gather momentum. Nashville, Arizona, North Carolina and Baltimore have provided fascinating and unique models, which could well be emulated.

6. **AFL Support**

The support of the International Committee of the AFL in cash and in kind must continue. There is no reason to assume that this will not occur. The AFL is very much aware of the vast resources of USA in relation to Australia's great game. We are approaching the time when full-time paid officials will be needed for the clubs in both coaching and performance. It will be interesting to see where the first breakouts occur in this regard because the quality of field play and administrative effort will explode.

7. **What leaps forwards can we expect?**

Semi-professionalization and visitations of super teams from Australia will soon occur. Even back in Carji Greeves' days in the 1920s business concerns employed him for promotional and skill development. There are enough successful Australian businessmen and women living in America to begin this charge even at this time. The spadework of convincing and conviction must occur. New forms of competition are already emerging. The Metro Leagues with different numbers of players on different sized fields are in evidence in several American cities. Once the college population (there are 9,000 universities and colleges in America) latches onto Australian Football, participation will explode. The sad fact of post-college inactivity after furious high school and college participation is a social problem within the States. Ethnic communities once they embrace the new game will enrich it enormously. The Irish community, the Italian community, the Black community, the Hispanic and the Asian communities have yet to discover USfooty. The prospect of support from these groups brings a smile to the faces of even the dourest of USfooty development officers.

8. **Jealousies**

One of the debilitating factors in institutional, corporate, communal and team existences is the ever-present perversion of interpersonal and inter group jealousies. When one looks at the contesting egos of faculty members in the most prestigious universities, one can understand why progress is impeded and joy is flattened with a sledgehammer. This scenario repeats itself in too many walks of life. Petty personal experiences have already intervened into the development of USfooty even in this short period of existence, but it has been controlled. It seems, too, that living in different territories, encourages parochial performance. The development of USfooty will need to battle through this problem if it is to be successful in establishing the potential might of this wonderful game.

9. **Looking Through the Peephole**

Peepholes are intriguing, difficult to resist, offering both surprising results and are hazardous to both the peerer and the peered. The authors invite readers of this book and fans of USfooty to offer their visions and predictions for the future. We see many recruits migrating to Australia and, in time, a test series played between Australia and the U.S. on a regular basis. The day will come when USfooty is financially larger than the AFL. The redoubtable Plugger dared the authors to finish this Chapter with the following scenario: "It was announced by the AFL in Melbourne last night, 20XX, that the financial rigors of world promotion were alleviated by two large grants from USfooty, suspected to be in the millions of dollars. AFL directors were relieved to endorse unilateral praise to the U.S. management companies who arranged these grants."

After reading this last injunction, Plugger O'Keeffe, ever the character, issued a personal challenge.

"I guarantee that at some time in the future USfooty will be financially larger than the AFL. I cannot say whether it will be in twenty, fifty or even one hundred years but it will happen. The U.S. sports market is enormous and already U.S. footy has an economic impact of around U.S.$5 million and that number will continue to grow exponentially. I may be labeled as a heretic but I was labeled in such fashion five years ago and look at what has happened. The gauntlet has been thrown to the next generation of administrators, players and supporters to pick up and prove me right."

Author "Doc" has this to add: "What an enterprise! The first five years of USfooty have been truly enjoyable, fascinating and eye-popping. These years and the ones that immediately follow are the best years in this enterprise. Soon clubs will grow, coaches will be hired, players from Australia will be exchanged and from other countries. Permanent grounds will develop and heavy financing will ensue. The nature of this game is such that crowds will eventually grow to spectate and cities will develop into hotbeds of parochial competition; e.g., The Boston Demons and The New York Magpies. Boston and New York have now enjoyed 350 years of intense rivalry. The Melbourne Demons and the Collingwood Magpies have enjoyed at least 100 years of intense rivalry. USfooty will simply add one more chapter to this story and all over these richly endowed fifty states, enterprises like USfooty will take their place.

Let it happen and long may it continue."

John "Doc" Cheffers
July 2003

Aylett, Allen, *My Game: A Life in Football As Told to Gregg Hobbs,* Sun Books, South Melbourne, 1986.

Barassi, Ron, with Peter McFarline, *Barassi: The Man Behind the Legend*, Simon and Schuster, Sydney, 1995.

Blainey, Geoffrey, *A Game of Our Own: The Origins of Australian Football*, National Australian Football Council, Information Australia, Melbourne, 1990.

Editors, John Press (Chief) et al, *100 Years of Australian Football, 1897-1996,* Penguin Books, Ringwood, Vic., 1996.

Flower, Robert with Ron Reed, *Robbie*, Caribou Publications, Melbourne, 1968.

Gordon, Harry, *The Hard Way: The Story of the Hawthorn Football Club,* Lester-Townsend Publishing, Sydney, 1990.

Hansen, Brian, *The Magpie Years '93,* Brian Hansen Publications, Cheltenham Vic.

Hutchinson, Col. *Cat's Tales: Geelong Football Club, 1897-1983,* Geelong Advertiser, 1984.

Matthews, Leigh with Mike Sheahan, *Lethal,* Caribou Publications, 1986.

Parkin, David, Ross Smith and Peter Schokman, *Premiership Football: How to Train, Play and Coach Australian Football,* Hargreen, North Melbourne, 1984.

Pascoe, Robert, *The Winter Game: The Complete History of Australian Football,* Text Publishing, Melbourne, 1995.

Richards, Lou and Tom Prior, *The Footballer Who Laughed,* Hutchinson of Australia, Richmond, Vic., 1981.

Web Page, http://www.uq.edu.au/`mlwham/banjo/index.html,
The Works of Banjo Paterson,
University of Queensland

USfooty Teams – A Sampling from the *Net*

Tucson Javelinas 2002-2003

Anthony "Squirrel" Starks - Club President

Jon "Sweets" Martinez - Club Vice-President

Jorge "Pimp Daddy" Pina - Webmaster

Rob "Blossom" Massey - Treasurer/Coach

Neil "DILF!!!!" Dilts

Ryan "Rhino" Starks

John Rascon

Patrick "Spongebob" McLaughlin

Robert "Mick" McGill

Brian Tarble

Kevin "Jeb" Brown

Allen "D&D" Campbell

R. "BOOOOOOOONE!!!" McLaughlin

George "Chef" Saliba

Toby "Circle-K"

Bruce "Airforce" Noble

Donnie "New Kid"

Denver Bulldogs

Cincinnati vs Atlanta Kookaburras 5/3/03

Cincinnati Dockers-Atlanta Kookaburras 6/3/02

Cincinnati Dockers and Atlanta Kookaburras battling for the ball

Milwaukee Bombers vs. Arizona Tournament

NY Magpies Division Champions Team 2001

New York Magpies Team 2003

Chicago Swans Junior Team competing against other junior teams in Australia May 2001

Chicago Swans Team

Western Pennsylvania Wallabies Team 2002

Western Pennsylvania Wallabies playing first ever game on May 18, 2002.

Austin Crows Team for TXAFL Metro Tournament

Excerpts from
Why the Boston Demons play away – Melbourne's *The Age* October 2, 1999

An American based football team embodies Australia's brain drain, writes **Geoff Strong**, who in giving permission for this excerpt used just three words. "*Go for it*"

Darren Louttit says the Australian rules football team he coaches is the smartest ever to have taken a mark. The photo that celebrates the end of last year's victorious season would appear to reinforce this boast. There are three professors, five other Ph.Ds plus five more players with masters degrees. Of the 33 in the picture, the only one without a degree is not an Australian. But don't expect to see the team play here – they are the Boston Demons, last year's United States Australian Football Association Champions .

Their success is Australian's loss. It is not so much that we miss their sporting skills – even Collingwood in wooden-spoon mode would probably thrash them. It is the loss of their minds that stands to hurt us most. In the team are three mathematicians and six scientists working on the cutting edge of biomedical research, including a team of three who are about to begin clinical trials on a new drug that could provide a cure for Alzheimer's disease.

Across most of the developed world, knowledge-based industries have driven economic growth, but Australia has lagged. If our best and brightest want a satisfying career with an income often many times what they would learn in Australia, the photo illustrates the best way to achieve it – go somewhere else, such as America.

Louttit, who grew up in East Bentleigh, played two seasons each for Melbourne and Fitzroy in the 1980s. He went to the US to work as an accountant. He says the picture represents "Australian's brain drain. This season we have so many Aussie expats wanting to play, we'll probably have to form two teams.".

A figure widely quoted in American scientific circles estimates that 90 per cent of that country's cutting edge research is undertaken by non-Americans. If it is true, much of the prosperity generated for America comes from brains that were educated elsewhere, but lured there by high salaries and generous research budgets. Australians are said to be in high demand due to the perceived quality of our education system. Even this might be under threat, warns Professor Fred Mendelsohn, head of the Howard Florey Institute of Medical Research.

Mendelsohn drew attention to the Boston Demons when he showed their team photo at The Age's recent Vision 21 seminar. He now fears shortsighted Government policies and a cultural distaste for intellectuals could be destroying the environment that nurtured people like this team. "We need an attitudinal change in this country. There is this culture of rugged individuality where we don't look up to the special talents of our best brains. "They are running down public teaching hospitals where our bright medical minds are being trained and there are also public education cutbacks to universities and schools. It is all shortsighted."

At the far left of the photo in the front row is Ashley Bush, Associate Professor of Psychiatry at Harvard Medical School and Director of the Laboratory for Oxidation Biology at the Genetics and Ageing Unit of the Massachusetts General Hospital. He grew up in Caulfield and St. Kilda and went to Mount Scopus College. Bush is one of the leaders of the international team of scientists that have developed the new Alzheimer's drug about to begin trials in Melbourne.

They have discovered a protein known as an amyloid, which accumulates in the brain as an insoluble deposit, drawing metals towards it. In the process the chemical hydrogen peroxide' is formed, which effectively bleaches the brain. A drug they have developed, called PRA3, has stopped and even reversed the process in laboratory animals and in dead human brains. If the trials are successful, a drug could be on the market within three years.

Bush, who went to the US on a Harkness Fellowship in 1992, laments the factors that have kept him overseas. He says that in the US a research scientist can earn three times the salary offered by a university in Australia.

In the US, Australian football teams must have at least eight American players on the field during a match, so this year the Demons have had to broaden their player base.

"Playing Aussie rules has been an eye-opener for many of the Yanks. It has become a beachhead for the concept of mateship," says Bush.

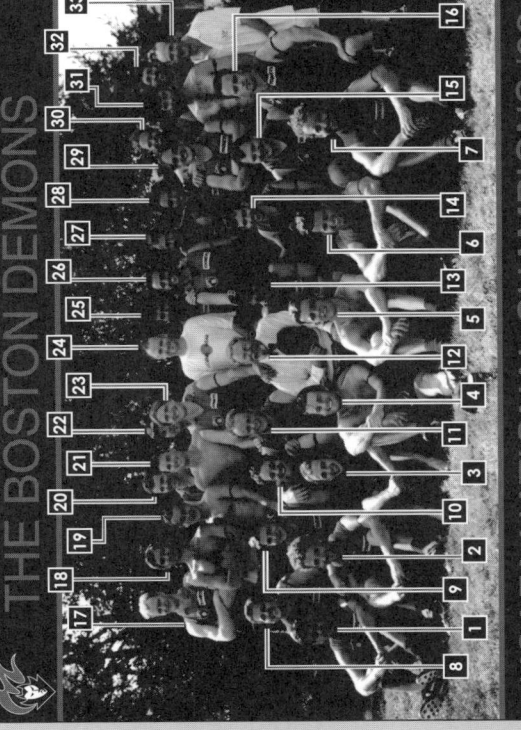

THE BOSTON DEMONS

USAFA NATIONAL CHAMPIONS '98

1. **Ashley Bush**, Associate Professor of Psychiatry, Harvard Medical School. Working on a cure for Alzheimer's Disease. From St. Kilda.

2. **Peter Dodds**, PhD, researcher for the Maths Department, Massachusetts Institute of Technology. From Horsham.

3. **Anthony Alembakis**, Masters degree in economics, financial controller. From Brunswick.

4. **Paul Clark**, Bachelor of accounting, auditor for accounting company, founding club president. From Doncaster.

5. **Scott McIntyre**, Bacheolor of marketing, travel industry. From Horsham.

6. **Andrew Bennett**, salesman hospital medical equipment. From Wonga Park

7. **Paul Whiting**, Masters degree computer science. From Essendon.

8. **Steven Gains**, Bachelor of marketing, sales for industrial supply company, American from Boston

9. Unknown

10. **Rob Moir**, PhD, neuroscientist working with Professor Bush studying Alzheimer's. From Perth.

11. **John Martin**, Bachelor of education, works developing software for Lotus. From Doncaster.

12. **John Cheffers**, professor of human movement Boston University, former Carlton player and former head of Australian Institute of Sport, author of 17 books. Patron and assistant coach. From Box Hill.

13. **Darren Loutit**, Bachelor of accounting, accountant, team coach, played for Melbourne and Fitzroy. From East Bentleigh.

14. **Craig Atwood**, PhD, researcher in neuroscience works with Professor Bush. From Perth

15. **John Roe**, American, one-eyed Collingwood supporter. Flew to Melbourne for the last game at Victoria Park. First saw game on cable TV. Works in Boston service station.

16. **Dean Jackman**, Bachelor of computer science, software architect. From Bendigo.

17. **Will Henwood**, Bachelor of accounting and Masters in marketing, accountant. From Perth.

18. **Andrew Blencowe** ("Psycho"), Bachelor of computer science, millionaire software developer, built football field behind house. From Moorabbin.

19. **Adrian Gleeson**, Bachelor of accounting, auditor. From Wonga Park.

20. **Adrian Purtschert**, Bachelor of accounting and Masters in finance, accountant. From Canberra.

21. **Brett Webster**, Bachelor of accounting, accountant, played North Melbourne Under 19s. From Armadale.

22. **Steve Budrick**, Revolution and Boston Demons trainer.

23. **Adam Mutton**, Bachelor of computer science, software developer, From East Doncaster.

24. **Rob Burgess**, Bachelor of physiotherapy, physiotherapist, played with Norwood South Australia. From Port Augusta.

25. **Anthony Slavin**, PhD in neuroscience, multiple sclerosis research at Harvard Hospital, From Essendon.

26. **Jim Thompson**, Masters in chemical engineering, chemical engineer, From Camberwell.

27. **Tom Ruyle**, American, Masters in biology, biological researcher.

28. **"Sideshow Bob"**, real name unknown. Victorian student, played one weekend.

29. **Colm** (surname unknown). Computer Scientist. From Irish university.

30. **Simon McClusky**, PhD in maths department, Massachusetts Institute of Technology. From Gosford New South Wales.

31. **Shane McHugh**, Bachelor of computer science, systems analyst. From Greensborough.

32. **Richard Stone**, professor of maths, Boston University. Son of former Senator John Stone. From Canberra.

33. **Ron Stux**, Umpire